To J P
You Are forever
a winner

Colin Grant.

FIGHTBACK
THE AUTOBIOGRAPHY OF GARY JACOBS

FIGHTBACK
THE AUTOBIOGRAPHY OF GARY JACOBS

**GARY JACOBS
WITH COLIN GRANT**

EMPIRE PUBLICATIONS

First published in 2025

This book is copyright under the Berne Convention. All rights are reserved. Apart from any fair dealing for the purpose of private study, research, criticism or review, as permitted under the Copyright Act, 1956, no part of this publication may be reproduced, stored in a retrieval system, or transmitted, in any form or by any means, electronic, electrical, chemical, mechanical, optical, photocopying, recording or otherwise, without the prior permission of the copyright owner. Enquiries should be sent to the publishers at the undermentioned address:

EMPIRE PUBLICATIONS
1 Newton Street, Manchester M1 1HW
© Gary Jacobs & Colin Grant 2025

ISBN: 9781915616173

Printed in Great Britain by Bell and Bain Ltd, Glasgow

Contents

About the Authors	1
The Man in the Van	3
Losing The Plot	6
I Belong to Glasgow	29
From Doncaster to Las Vegas	44
As Seen on TV	66
George Collins	75
Into the Deep End	82
Chris Eubank And Schoolboy Scraps	90
Under New Management	103
A Fresh Start	113
My Mentor	124
French Toast	145
Betting the Farm	151
Nervous but Determined	161
A Sickening Night	180
Making the Weight	186
Dunkirk Spirit	192
Hanging up the Gloves	197
The Fightback	205
Still Fighting	210

This book is dedicated in loving memory of Maurice Lewis.

About the Authors

GARY JACOBS was a highly-successful boxer from Glasgow. During a 12-year career he held the Scottish, British, Commonwealth and European Welterweight championships. He won 45 of his 53 pro fights and lost a world title bid on points to an opponent described as 'the world's best pound for pound boxer'.

COLIN GRANT has worked as a journalist in Glasgow for many years. He interviewed Gary at the start of his professional boxing journey and the two have been friends ever since.

Acknowledgements

THE AUTHORS WOULD LIKE to acknowledge the great gratitude they owe to the following people who contributed to this book: Mike Barret, Diarmid Bruce, Alan Buchanan, Stewart Cosgrove, Dave Douglas, Mickey Duff, Chris Eubank, Tom Fitzsimmons, Linda Jacobs, Bobby Keddie, Rosemary Lewis, Jeff Lim, Timothy Lovat, John McDermott, Alex McDonald, Tom McHarry, Peter McLean, Gary Mann, Alan Morris, Ian Mullholand, Martin Newman, Jack Owens, Dean Powell, Syd Rose, Graham Sulkin and Ian Wilson.

The Man in the Van

IT WAS A COLD, grey Glasgow November morning on the Erskine Bridge high above the water. Nearby, an old blue Renault Clio was parked. A man sat fidgeting in the driver's seat smoking his ninth cigarette of the day, even though it was only half-past ten.

Glancing nervously at his watch every so often, he fiddled anxiously with the gold wedding ring on his finger. As passers-by rushed or ambled past, he was grateful for the steamed-up windows which obscured his face. The last thing he wanted was to be spotted, although he knew he was only delaying the inevitable for a very short time.

Another glance at the watch was followed by an exhalation of smoke which doubled for a long weary sigh. It was time to get it over and done with. Pulling his hoodie tighter to his head he stepped out, hunched into the wind and into himself.

It was blowy on the bridge, hundreds of feet above a grey and rippling River Clyde. He looked down and wondered for the thousandth time how he had ended up in this desolate place.

He fleetingly thought about the absurdity of his situation. He was standing at the highest point for miles, yet he knew he'd reached rock bottom. For him at any rate it just didn't get any worse than this. He'd been hurt before, yet had never experienced such pain. The fanfare, bright lights and pretty girls were all gone, replaced by private shame and public humiliation. He realised how easy it would be to make his demons disappear. It would take just a very short time to hit the water and his troubles would be over in an instant.

All these images were racing through his head, but they came to an abrupt halt when a passing white van slowed down and someone inside shouted, "Don't dae it!". As he turned to respond the van drove off so he'll never know who uttered those fateful words or why but he'll always be grateful to whoever it was. The shout had disrupted the waves of self-pity which had engulfed him that miserable morning.

As he stood there more confused than ever it suddenly felt very cold. He longed for warmth. The impulse to jump off had gone.

As he trudged back to the car it dawned on him that for a while now he had forgotten one of the most important tenets of his life. All these terrible things were destroying him and his family, mainly due to his own lack of judgement, yet he hadn't lifted a finger to prevent them from happening.

He had thrown in the towel, and that wasn't him.

At that moment something changed inside him. He knew he couldn't just give up. He had a choice. He could be brave again. He could fight back.

The next day he entered a nondescript government building in the South Side of Glasgow and waited his turn to sign on. A number of men nearby glanced over at him, some with curiosity, others in amazement. One muttered to the other: "Whit's Gary Jacobs daein' here?"

Gary looked over and replied with a weak smile, "Same as you, pal. I'm fucked."

Gary's was an amazing fall from grace. As a boxer he was one of the best, having been British, European and Commonwealth champion. He'd earned millions and lived the high life and when he retired he was financially secure, but now he'd lost everything; his home, money, business and dignity.

His was not the classic boxing rags-to-riches-to-rags story. Rather, it was riches-to-beyond-your-wildest-dreams-riches...

To rags.

He was brought up in a middle-class Jewish family who

lived in relatively affluent surroundings. His father was a successful businessman with his own firm.

His parents always owned their home and the family, Gary and his twin brother and sister, lacked for nothing.

Gary went to some of the best state schools in Scotland where, by all accounts, he did well. Growing up he excelled in many sports he also enjoyed playing chess.

This is the story of his rise and fall and of his courageous, ongoing, fight back.

This is his story.

Losing The Plot

SINCE LEAVING SCHOOL I'd always been in work. Now, for the first time in my adult life, I was without a job. I hadn't made any public statement about my future but I knew deep down my boxing career was over.

And I needed to find something to do with my time, otherwise I'd go crazy. Finances weren't an issue. I'd earned well and had managed to hold on to quite a bit of my prize money. Linda and I had a nice big house with no mortgage and money in the bank. But I liked to keep busy, either working or training.

There was no hint of the destructive tsunami which would soon engulf me and my family for several years.

I was still happy and successful at this point and delighted when, in October 1997, Sky TV asked me to commentate on the forthcoming Lennox Lewis-Andrew Golota WBC heavyweight title fight.

I had done some TV work before, for the various channels, but at that time I was still first and foremost a professional boxer. I was now hoping to forge a new career behind the microphone and this would be a good way to start.

Unfortunately, there wasn't much of an opportunity for me to display my deep knowledge and vast understanding of the fight game because Lennox KO'd his challenger halfway through the first round. A great insight wasn't required to explain what had happened here.

Nevertheless, Sky came back with more offers for my ringside analysis and I was beginning to enjoy the new role. The money wasn't great compared to what I was used to but it was an income. I was working alongside the likes of Barry McGuigan and we developed a strong friendship.

Lewis and Golota had one thing in common – they had both appeared on the undercard when I was in my prime. Golota had fought on the night of my unsuccessful world title bid against Pernell Whitaker on 26th August 1995.

As I was making final preparations for the biggest night of my career, Golota demolished West Turner in just 17 seconds of the first round to continue his unbeaten progress towards a first title fight. It was his 25th win and 21st KO.

He would soon star as a villain in one of the most infamous fights in modern boxing history, while his opponent on that shameful night would eventually become yet another tragic victim of the sport.

Golota had represented Poland at the 1988 Olympics in Seoul and won a bronze, but in 1990 he got into a bar-room brawl which left another man badly beaten up. He faced five years in jail if found guilty of assault, so Golota skipped town and re-emerged in the USA, which became his home.

Less than 12 months after beating Turner, on 11th July 1996, he got the first of his four cracks at the world heavyweight title, when he took on WBO champion Riddick Bowe in Madison Square Gardens.

During the opening rounds it was obvious the challenger was on top. Golota's punching was far more effective and after three rounds he was comfortably ahead. Yet for some inexplicable reason, Golota had started hitting the champ below the belt. Referee Wayne Kelly gave him a public warning after his first low blow in the second round, and a second warning after Golota did it again in the third. In the fourth round Golota dropped Bowe with yet another low blow and this time Kelly deducted a point from him.

Golota dominated the fight against a very unconvincing champ but in the seventh he landed another painful illegal blow which cost him an additional point. At this point ref Kelly issued Golota with a final warning, stating any more contact below the belt would lead to automatic disqualification.

Incredibly, just before the bell to end the round Golota battered Bowe in his testes yet again and the ref had no option but to stop the fight, disqualify the Pole and awarding the win to the champion. Suddenly all hell broke loose. Within seconds of the stoppage, a group of Bowe's security team entered the ring and one started pushing Golota who retaliated by punching him. As the scuffle continued in a packed ring, another of Bowe's men hit Golota in the head with a walkie-talkie and the resulting cut needed 11 stitches. Chaos reigned and Golota's trainer, 74-year-old Lou Duva, who had managed 19 world champions, collapsed with chest pains and was taken out on a stretcher.

By now both sets of fans in the 11,000-plus crowd had joined in and a mass brawl inside and outside the ring ensued. One of the ringside TV commentators was the reigning IBF and WBU world heavyweight champ George Foreman. He saved two of his fellow commentators from fans who had attacked them. The riot raged for over 30 minutes before more than 150 police officers, backed up by the venue's security, restored order.

When the dust settled a dozen fans had been taken to hospital, a similar number of police officers needed treatment for injuries and 10 arrests were made.

Despite the scandal, the stage was set for a rematch, and it came just five months later in December 1996. Incredibly, it was a rerun of their first encounter with Golota taking control against an under-performing Bowe then being disqualified for low blows. Although both boxers earned millions of dollars for their performances, neither fighter recovered from these shameful scenes.

I was commentating at Golota's next fight, when Lennox knocked him out inside two minutes. Three years later the Pole was offered another big payday against Mike Tyson, which descended into another highly controversial affair. After just two rounds Golota refused to fight any further and the referee was forced to declare Tyson the winner. Tests later showed he had a broken bone in his head, which might have caused serious internal damage had he continued. Golota alluded that the damage might have come from regular headbutting by Tyson. Meanwhile, Tyson tested positive for marijuana, so instead of winning by a TKO the fight was declared "No Contest."

It would be three years before Golota's next fight, but by then he was a spent force.

Riddick Bowe's career spiralled downwards even quicker after the two Golota fiascos. He initially retired from boxing to join the Marine Corps. But his new career as a tough soldier lasted just three days before he quit and headed home from training camp. Next, he faced accusations of beating up his sister. His strange behaviour continued when he kidnapped his estranged wife and children at knifepoint. When he arrived at her home in North Carolina he threatened her with a knife, handcuffs, duct tape, and pepper spray. He forced her and their five children into a car and set off for his Maryland home. At one stage Bowe stopped the car at a McDonald's and his wife managed to evade him long enough to call her sister. Police arrived within minutes, and Bowe was arrested and jailed for 18 months. His strange actions are thought to be a consequence of brain damage suffered in the ring during a stellar career which ended with 43 wins and just one defeat.

During my short-lived TV career, one of the most memorable fights I worked on was the 1997 WBC Super Bantam title fight between Daniel Zaragosa and Wayne McCullough. Mexican Zaragosa won by a split decision and I agreed with this because he was hitting a little bit harder than the Belfast-born McCullough was used to. The drama spilled over to the post-fight TV interview with the champion. A McCullough fan started shouting about the Irishman being robbed and HBO's Larry Merchant smashed him with a right hook which sent him flying! Then the commentator brushed himself down and continued his conversation with Zaragosa as if nothing had happened!

By then I'd become a personal trainer to a small number of wealthy, but unfit, businessmen and women in Glasgow. I still enjoyed going through the exercise routines and I began looking for ways to expand this line of work. Eventually, after a great deal of time weighing up the pros and cons, I decided to open my own upmarket fitness centre. I still don't know what possessed me to reach this conclusion. For a start, I knew nothing about running a business. But, as usual, I was full of confidence and determination and I liked being in control of my own affairs so this 'minor' inconvenience was cast aside.

And I had plenty of money. There was approximately £120,000 in the bank and enough equity in our four-bedroom luxury villa to enable me to borrow a further £100,000. In addition to all that I was promised backing to the tune of £150,000 from a wealthy businessman who I considered a friend.

Armed with all this financial clout I merrily and blindly began turning my plans into reality. Yet, without realising it, I had stumbled into a minefield and had embarked upon a course of action that would end in tragedy, with terrible consequences for me and my family.

It didn't take long to find premises, above the Iceland store in Kilmarnock Road, Shawlands, in the South Side of Glasgow. I wanted "The Gary Jacobs Health and Fitness Club" to be better than anything available in the city at that time and set about identifying the latest fitness machines on the market.

They were expensive, as was kitting out the premises, but I reckoned the investment would be worth it from a business perspective. In any event, I had plenty of money, or so I thought. However, as the gym took shape costs began to mount and my pot of cash was diminishing at an alarming rate. Despite that, I was comforted by the knowledge that it really was looking good and there was plenty of interest from potential members.

Shortly before completion in 1999 the first disaster struck. My so-called pal, the wealthy businessman who had promised financial backing, pulled out of the project. A few days later I woke up to the fact that unless I immediately paid the builder £30,000, he wouldn't finish the job. If that happened the gym would never open and I would lose everything. Yet I had exhausted all my money. I had nothing left. It was my biggest nightmare. At least I thought it was. Little did I realise there was much worse to come.

At this stage I had a junior partner in the business. Alex McDonald was a good lightweight who was content fighting in the amateur ranks. We had met while playing for Scotland's most famous charity football team, Dukla Pumpherston, and had become pals.

Alex ran a pub in Plean, near Stirling, and was keen to get involved in the gym. He had contributed a substantial sum at the start of the project so he, too, stood to lose his investment if work wasn't completed. With nowhere else to turn, he approached his businessman father-in-law, John Dougal, for a loan that would pay the builder and it came as a great relief to us both when he agreed.

We had to promise to repay him within eight weeks and although that seemed a little on the quick side to me, we had no other option. And John's money got the gym open.

Right from the first day the business took off and the list of members who were prepared to pay £30 a month grew rapidly. Within six months we had around 500 on our books. Yet we never seemed to have any spare money. The running costs swallowed up almost everything. And we still hadn't repaid John Dougal. In fact, we'd gone back to him and borrowed more to maintain cash flow.

I had been running the company and it was clear I was way

out of my depth. So, in desperation, we hired a professional manager, who'd come highly recommended by a friend, and I took on more of a marketing role. We got a few more members on the books but the financial position didn't improve.

I had been taking a salary and I could justify that because I worked in the gym every day, assisting members with their training plans. Alex, meanwhile, hadn't received a penny.

The new structure wasn't working and we parted company with our manager, but that didn't solve our problems. Our debts continued to spiral and we didn't know what to do about it. Then another pal recommended a business consultant friend of his and, clutching at straws, I went to see him.

One thing led to another and eventually in early 2001 I agreed to sign the business over to his company, Track Globe Ltd. In return, I would receive a small payment and be kept on as the day-to-day manager.

I am, even now, far from convinced this arrangement was in my best interests. However, I signed the paperwork with my eyes open and have no complaints. I do regret that Alex McDonald lost his money as well but at the time I couldn't see an alternative.

I'd stubbornly believed in being master of my own destiny. I was full of confidence about my own abilities, which is why I launched this venture in the first place.

I was also very proud of myself and what I had achieved. For those reasons I decided not to seek advice from any number of Jewish accountants and lawyers I had known over the years in the South Side of Glasgow. I would make the decisions without their help. I now realise it was a big mistake but at the time I couldn't bring myself to admit it. I was also hoping to solve all my problems with as few people as possible finding out. I didn't want anybody to know that for the first time in my life I was a failure. And what a colossal failure! Opening the health club cost me over £200,000, much of it borrowed. Now I'd lost the lot.

Looking back on those dark days it is clear I was living in denial. I had an image to project to the world and nothing was going to interfere with that. Only a short time earlier I had been a highly-successful professional boxer. I enjoyed the fame and fortune that came my way. I had a group of happy-go-lucky friends who were always going on exciting holidays and turning up at the most fashionable night clubs. I had an open invitation to accompany them at their expense.

In turn, they enjoyed being seen in my company. But I took my craft seriously and only rarely ventured out with them. I liked the limelight (who wouldn't?) but my training came first and I neither drank nor smoked. Now, as my business began to fall apart, I felt more than ever the need to maintain the façade of success. So, with a new set of pals, I began going out more and soon became a regular fixture at some of Glasgow's top pubs and clubs.

I didn't see it but one obvious indicator of the immense stress I was under was the fact I had started smoking again. I had been a smoker before I became a boxer. Another clue was that I had, for the first time in my life, turned to drink.

The cost of all this late-night socialising was met by my mates, who were more than happy to fork out for the status and thrill of hanging out with a famous ex-pro.

Money was tight. No doubt about it. I was still commentating on Sky, while I received around £15,000 when I handed over my gym to the new owners and a salary for being the face of the business. One day I lost that income too. I turned up for work at the gym to be denied entry by a couple of burly security guards. When I protested that I was the manager they said: "Not anymore you're not!" It was another brutal blow to my self-esteem but the seriousness of my situation still hadn't hit me. Things would get a whole lot worse before I woke up.

Linda, at home bringing up our three young children, was blissfully unaware of the impending doom. Throughout our marriage she'd known only success and a good standard of living. Then when I came up with the plans for the gym she got excited. Of course, I had to tell her I'd sold the gym but I kept the full gory details from her. The intermittent cheques from Sky helped but I was forced to start selling some of my prized possessions to pay the bills. I'd amassed a collection of expensive motorcycles and luxury watches and one by one they had to go. Although they fetched nearly £40,000, our life was beginning to unravel.

Despite that, I acted as if I hadn't a care in the world. I had no regular income, massive debts and precious few ideas of how to make money, but I carried on partying and clubbing with my pals. We struggled on for the next year or so, with our debts gradually increasing. Then came another bombshell – the calls from Sky stopped coming.

Around that time rumours had begun circulating in Glasgow that I was mixed up with the drug scene in the city. It was true that some of the new friends I'd made since quitting the ring were regular cocaine users and it is also true that I was in their company when that happened. However, it was untrue, at this point, to suggest I was joining in. That particular recreational pursuit would become a major part of my life one day, but not at that moment.

One embarrassing late-night incident made headlines and probably influenced Sky's decision. In October 2002 the papers reported that I had been kicked out of a Glasgow nightclub and there was a suggestion that I had been taking drugs. According to the papers, toilet attendants at Tiger Tiger spotted a clubber snorting cocaine in the gents and raised the alarm. I was with a group of pals from London and we were all asked to leave. I don't know who was taking drugs, it certainly wasn't me, but it must have been someone in our crowd.

I protested to the management about our treatment and because I was still a bit of a minor celeb, the papers got to hear about it. When contacted by a reporter I stated: "I have never taken any cocaine and I never would." Although true at the time, those words would come back to haunt me before long. The result was that I'd lost my last income stream. This was yet another hammer blow but, compared to some of the problems I'd faced recently, it wasn't the worst piece of news.

To many people my position would appear pretty hopeless, but it was nowhere near as disastrous as the crisis that was slowly but steadily escalating in the background and would soon overwhelm me.

By January 2003, a month after my 37th birthday, almost every penny Linda and I ever had was gone. Matters came to a head that month when East Renfrewshire Council demanded just over £7000 for unpaid Council Tax stretching back five years. We couldn't afford to settle the bill so the council went to Paisley Sheriff Court to declare us bankrupt. Now at this point all was not lost because we had some equity in our house. The bank, which held our mortgage, was very understanding and allowed us to sell the property.

Things were descending from bad to worse but I was still a long way from rock bottom.

There was no money coming in to the household. Life had turned upside down. The house didn't sell right away and Linda became increasingly upset and resentful about our situation. In the meantime, she got a part-time job which provided our only income.

It was around this time that I finally succumbed to the lure of cocaine. The impending loss of the house, and all the other issues, began to sink in and the drug offered me a way to block out the pain. It made the badness disappear. I had plenty of pals who were happy to keep me supplied, either free of charge or for very little cost.

Unfortunately for my bewildered family, I soon began to adopt a cocaine lifestyle. I'd go out and drink, do drugs and party all night long before coming home in the morning and sleeping on the sofa till lunchtime. I'd wake up for a bite to eat then fall asleep again till dinner time. I'd sleep on for a few more hours then get washed and changed before heading out into the night to meet my mates for another round of partying fuelled by alcohol and drugs.

My erratic existence soon led to more unwanted publicity. In June 2003 I was kicked out of a nightclub called Cube after an argument with the stewards. A report in a Sunday paper described me as "emotional" and added that my friends had become increasingly concerned about my lifestyle.

The article stated: "Jacobs is a regular in Glasgow's clubland, despite being married to wife Linda and father of three young children. Just a few years ago he was one of Scotland's sporting heroes, carrying the nation's hopes of a world title into the ring. But now the skint ex-champ's reputation is on the ropes."

Linda's pals started asking her about my behaviour, with some suggesting to her I was hooked on drugs. She also noticed that I had become comfortable with alcohol. Throughout my career I had been presented with various bottles of spirits, mainly whisky, to celebrate a victory or an award. Since I didn't drink and Linda never touched spirits, some were given away as gifts but many remained untouched in a large sideboard in the lounge for years.

As my depression deepened, I began to surreptitiously raid the sideboard. Linda told me years later she had turned a blind eye to my secretive activities in the hope they would go away.

The villa was eventually sold. We got a good price for it, paid off our debt to the Council, kept a little for ourselves and prepared to move out.

Our new home was a small rented flat not far from where we'd been living. It took Linda some time to come to terms with the prospect of losing the house. It had always been busy, full of people. The children, who'd been born there, loved running about, enjoying the space and playing with the dog. It was a proper family home, full of warmth. The two-bedroom flat we moved into was tiny by comparison and although we struggled to pay the rent every month I was still lost in a decadent world of drink, drugs and partying.

By July my love of the nightlife led to a more serious incident. I'd driven into town then gone clubbing with my pals. As we left the club I went to my car, which was parked in Queen Street, to collect my jacket.

I'd had plenty to drink. As I got back out the car a couple of police officers challenged me. They claimed that my actions amounted to being in charge of the vehicle and they attempted to breathalyse me. I refused on the grounds that I hadn't been driving and had no intention of doing so. My protests fell on deaf ears and I was arrested and taken to Stewart Street police station. When I was searched police found a match box in my pocket containing a couple of Ecstasy tablets, which led to me being charged with possession of a Class A drug and with failing to provide a breath test.

The episode led to a furious row with Linda. She was woken at 5am by a phone call from police advising her of my whereabouts and asking her to come and pick me up. She had to phone her sister and get her to drive round to our flat where she picked up Linda and our three sleepy-eyed children. They all arrived at Stewart Street and Linda drove us all home. She was fuming and I said very little. She tried to quiz me but I just brushed it off and blamed the cops for getting it all wrong. That night, after sleeping for most of the day, I went out clubbing again as if nothing had happened! Eventually, the authorities decided to drop the drugs charges, while I agreed to plead guilty to the motoring offence and received a year's driving ban.

As Linda and the children tried hard to lead a normal life, which involved going to work and getting to school on time, I was, incredibly, still cocooned in my own little self-indulgent world.

One day, late in 2003, everything I'd been blocking out of my head for years suddenly hit me like a hurricane. I was no longer the great Gary Jacobs, living the high life with my name up in lights. I was an insignificant nobody with no money and no prospects. I'd endured years of pain and put my life in danger to earn a small fortune and now I'd lost everything, including my pride. I was a junkie and a heavy drinker scrambling around to keep a roof over my family's head.

I'd given it all away.

And now the only way out was to do the unthinkable and ask the state for help. I would need to join the many others who were down on their luck and sign on. This really was rock bottom. And I just couldn't take it any longer. So I did the first thing that entered my head and drove to Erskine Bridge.

It was Sunday, a typical Glasgow November morning - cold, and grey. In a car park not far from the Bridge, I sat and fidgeted in my old, blue Renault Clio.

It was only half-past ten but I was already on my ninth cigarette of the day. Every so often I glanced nervously at my watch, a present from Linda, and fiddled anxiously with the gold wedding ring on my finger.

As passers-by rushed or ambled past the car I was grateful for the steamed-up windows which obscured my image. The last thing I wanted was to be spotted, although I knew I was only delaying the inevitable for a very short time. An exhalation of smoke doubled for a long weary sigh. I got out the car, pulled my hoodie tighter to my head and hunched into the wind, and into myself.

It was blowy on the bridge, hundreds of feet above a grey and rippling River Clyde. I looked down and wondered for the thousandth time how I had ended up in this desolate place. It just didn't get any worse than this. I'd been hurt before yet had never experienced such pain. The fanfare, bright lights and pretty girls were all gone, replaced by private shame and public humiliation.

I realised how easy it would be to make my demons disappear. It would take just a very short time to hit the water and my troubles would be over in an instant.

All these thoughts were racing through my head, but they came to an abrupt halt when a passing white van slowed down and someone inside shouted, "Don't Dae It!"

As I turned to respond the van drove off so I'll never know who uttered those fateful words or why. But I'll always be grateful to whoever it was. He had disrupted the waves of self-pity which had enveloped me that miserable morning.

As I stood there more confused than ever, it suddenly felt very cold. I longed for warmth. The impulse to jump had gone. As I trudged back to the car it dawned on me that for a while now I had forgotten one of the most important tenets of my life. All these terrible things were harming me and my family, mainly due to my own lack of judgement, yet I hadn't lifted a finger to prevent them from happening.

I had thrown in the towel.

At that moment something changed inside me. I knew I couldn't just give up. I had a choice. I could be brave again. I could fight back.

The next day I entered a nondescript building in the South Side of Glasgow and waited my turn. A number of men nearby glanced over at me, some with curiosity, others in amazement. One plucked up the courage to ask, "Whit are you daein on the dole?" I looked over and replied with a weak smile, "Same as you pal. I'm fucked."

I signed on for a few months, then got some work with a removal firm and for the next year or so we were all pretty happy. Although I had found it easy to stop taking drugs and cut out the alcohol, I couldn't quit smoking – a habit that clings to me to this day.

But my party days were over and I, belatedly, became a

typical family man. The children, who'd once had their own bedrooms, now shared one between them. But they were delighted to be at the same school with the same pals. I knew from bitter experience how important that small measure of stability would be for them.

But nothing lasts forever and we were soon on the move again. The lease period had come to an end and the landlord wanted the flat back so he and his wife could move in.

Our next home was a big, detached house round the corner. We were still renting and money was coming in, although not as regularly as I would have liked. I couldn't keep a job for long because I instinctively objected to being told what to do. I had always been fiercely independent, which is what initially attracted me to boxing. My view was, "I don't work for you, I work with you." Looking back I know my attitude was at best immature and at worst irresponsible, but I just hated being bossed around.

The rent on the new place was high but I could just about handle it and Linda and the kids loved the extra space. After a year the lease was up and the landlord had plans for the property and wanted us out. It was important for us to stay in the area so we moved into a two-bedroom flat round the corner.

This time there was just not enough room for the five of us. It was hellish. We had to get out. Unfortunately, by now I had pissed off too many employers. I wasn't working and we never had enough money to pay the bills. I had to go back on benefits. The cheques came in every month and most of the time it paid the rent. Occasionally, however, the temptation to use the housing money to pay for ordinary everyday living expenses was too great.

Inevitably, we fell behind with the rent and I had to sell my car to pay off debts. It was an old banger, all I could afford. The days of running around in brand new Porsches had long since gone. But I used the cash to cover two months' rent arrears.

Life was tough and all Linda and I could see on the horizon were dark clouds. Yet, in the depths of our despair, incredibly and unbeknown to us, our luck was about to change for the better.

Timothy Lovat is 12 years younger than me and a highly-successful businessman. He is also one of my biggest fans. However, because of the age gap I didn't know anything about him. But I soon got to know a great deal.

It transpired that as he was growing up in Newton Mearns, not far from the first home Linda and I shared, my exploits in and out of the ring were one of the main conversation topics at the traditional Friday night dinner, which is one of the cultural highlights in most Jewish homes.

To many Jews in Glasgow I was a hero and I certainly was to Tim. When we eventually met he told me I was the most famous guy he knew. He said some mornings when he was being driven to school, he'd pass me out on a training run and he couldn't wait to tell his mates in the playground that he'd seen the great Jewish boxer. He reminded me of the one and only time we'd previously met. It was at a social event at a local golf club. His dad knew me and introduced us.

As a youngster Tim shared some of my traits. He liked to stand up for himself and was always getting into fights. At school he often protected his two brothers if they were being bullied, so his dad asked me if Tim would make a good boxer. At this point Tim was a chubby teenager. Apparently, I asked to see his muscles, gave his arm a feel and told him he needed to go to the gym a bit more.

Meeting his hero was a very exciting moment for Tim, but not one I remember to be honest.

Tim wasn't a fight fan and our paths never crossed again, even though we lived two minutes away from each other, until I opened the gym. By now he'd joined the family business and the gym was 100 yards from his office. His father was one of the first to join and he also arranged membership for the whole family. To begin with Tim trained once or twice a month and every so often we'd see each other. Then, when I lost the business, Tim and his brother Robin stopped going.

I didn't realise it at the time but the two-bedroom Newton Mearns flat we now rented belonged to his family. And when I fell massively behind with the rent, it presented Tim with a terrible dilemma. Under normal circumstances he would go through a process of trying to get to the root of the tenants' problems and, if that didn't bear fruit, eviction proceedings would begin. Eventually, once he'd gone to court he would serve the eviction notice.

But this was different. I was his hero and he couldn't bring himself to treat me like any other bad tenant. Tim knew I was going through tough times and he didn't want to make matters worse for me and my family.

Tim and his father, who ran a property company, agonised over my predicament. They concluded they would do everything they could to recover the missing money from me, but if it came to the crunch they would not evict my family. Basically, they decided to help me out.

The decision was made easier because they owned the property. Had they been acting for another owner then they would have had to put the owner's best interests first – and may not have been able to help me in this way.

It was a life-changing moment for me and it happened without my knowledge.

One day, about a year later, Tim created another life-changing moment for me. By now I knew he was my landlord.

He phoned me out of the blue because he needed a fridge moved from one flat to the other. None of the regular guys he employed were available. He offered me the job. I was very happy to accept and afterwards he paid me £50.

I must have impressed him because over the next few months he gave me more and more work, usually moving furniture from one property to another or delivering new appliances. This work continued on an occasional basis for a while before Tim offered me a contract. My job involved clearing rubbish bins in private flats the company managed in the East End of Glasgow. The job description was 'Refuse Management' and Tim admitted to me it was a strange feeling asking 'the great man' as he regarded me, to carry out such a menial task, yet I took on the job without hesitation. It was part of my comeback, not a come down as some people might see it.

Tim must have been impressed by my efforts because before long he required the same service for flats in the West End of the city so he gave me that contract to me as well. By now I'd begun employing people and was earning enough to afford to move into a bigger flat round the corner. We had spare cash and I began paying back the rent arrears – and the debt, which ran into thousands, was soon cleared.

About a year later Tim was negotiating with a contractor who cleaned some of his flats. They couldn't agree on a price so I stepped in and offered to do it for a lower fee. Tim pointed out to me that this was a major contract which required strong management skills, but I was unperturbed. I knew I could handle it and assured Tim. He wasn't totally convinced but agreed to him awarding me the contract on a trial basis. I went out and recruited staff and started a few days later. Once again, I was true to my word and the contract was mine permanently. I soon employed three teams of cleaners for all the flats I was looking after on Tim's behalf and was looking to expand the business to work with (not for!) other landlords.

Thanks to Tim's faith in me I was by now running a thriving wee firm and employing Linda who, graciously, had forgiven me for all my past indiscretions. Between us we'd been through a lot, but we had managed to stand up to the physical and emotional demands that came our way.

Suddenly, life was no longer a struggle and for the first time in a long time I didn't feel the need to fight back.

Life was good.

Well, it was.

For a few years.

Even the sudden and tragic death of my mentor Maurice Lewis in 2007 didn't keep me down for long.

Maurice had always looked after himself and in his late 60s was still a regular swimmer. In his younger days he'd swam competitively and even now he swam more than once a week.

On the night of 15th of February, 2007 he was relaxing in the sitting room of his Shawlands flat. He'd not long got back from the pool. His wife Rosemary was with him.

By now, aged 69, he was pretty much retired. He still had a few clients who sought his advice when buying jewellery, but he really didn't need to work for a living. He did it more for fun.

As he sat reading a paper with a cup of tea he suddenly pointed to his chest and told Rosemary: "I've got a pain."

She was an experienced nurse who worked at the local Victoria Infirmary and knew right away it was serious.

She gave him an aspirin and dialled 999.

Paramedics arrived very quickly, but Maurice was slipping away.

He was lifted onto an ambulance and rushed to the Victoria. Medics worked on him during the short journey and when they arrived. But they couldn't save him.

His funeral took place on Sunday 18th February at Glenduffhill, a Jewish cemetery in the East End of Glasgow. I'm pleased to say the boxing fraternity turned out in force to give him a big send-off.

He was a very special man and he made my career what it was. Without him and Rosemary I would never have got into a ring and I owe him everything. As you will see, it was Rosemary who first nudged me towards a career in boxing.

It took me a good while to get his passing out of my system, although my memories of him and the great times we enjoyed together will never leave me, life has to go on and I still had a family to look after, so I couldn't dwell on Maurice's death for too long.

I was still feeling numb but remained focused on hard work and business began to pick up again.

Before long Linda and I came to the conclusion that we'd got over the bad times. We congratulated ourselves and celebrated for battling through the dark days and getting on an even keel.

Then, out of the blue, something terrible happened. It was so nasty, it made everything we'd suffered so far seem like a Sunday school picnic.

In September 2010 Linda discovered a mark which resembled an indentation on her right breast. She didn't think it was important, although her best pal, Paula, urged her to see her GP.

Eventually, in late January 2011, she made an appointment at our local surgery, but the doctor couldn't find anything wrong. She reassured Linda there was nothing to worry about, but just before the end of the consultation, the GP asked Linda how she would feel about going to the breast clinic where they would carry out a mammogram just to be on the safe side. She made it clear it was just an option and the choice was entirely Linda's. She was about to say 'no' when something made her change her mind. She reckoned it wouldn't do any harm and would rule out anything serious once and for all.

And even though she agreed to go, her GP reassured her there was nothing to worry about.

She didn't get an appointment for ages and was told it would probably be sometime in April. So clearly there was no rush. At the start of April she got a call from the hospital. She was given the choice of an appointment later that month or in May. Linda decided to put it off till May because we were going to a friend's 50th birthday celebrations in London and there might have been a clash of dates. There was no real sense of urgency. May arrived and by the 18th she realised she hadn't heard from the hospital.

At 9.05 that day, just after arriving at work, she decided to check with the hospital. Neither of us will ever forget what happened next. The receptionist offered her a consultation at 10.30. There had been a cancellation. She went downstairs and asked her boss if she could get away for an hour or so at most to go to the nearby Victoria Hospital. When he agreed she phoned Paula and asked her to meet her there. The pair of them sat in the waiting room giggling and laughing about some other pals, without a care in the world. As far as Linda was concerned there was nothing to fear.

The consultant examined her and said he couldn't feel anything untoward but decided to send her for a mammogram just to be on the safe side. After the mammogram she was sent back to the waiting room. A few minutes later a nurse appeared and announced that Linda needed to go for an ultrasound scan. Linda wondered why she needed a scan on top of the mammogram, but it was a fleeting thought.

Paula, though, was unnerved. Although she didn't say anything at the time, she later told Linda she was getting very worried by this turn of events. As Linda entered the room the nurse asked her if she was feeling OK and if she had anyone with her. Linda nonchalantly confirmed she was fine and that her pal was in the waiting room.

Even at this point she was completely unconcerned. She reckoned the nurse was just being thorough. The ultrasound exam was carried out. Then the nurse dropped the bombshell: "We've seen something on the mammogram and now we're seeing it on the ultrasound. If you don't mind, we'd like to carry out a biopsy. We could do it today."

A stunned Linda gave the go ahead and was administered anaesthetic.

Unfortunately, she wasn't given enough and when the first

of five biopsies was done she was in a great deal of pain. Next the consultant returned, accompanied by a specialist. They gave her the worst possible news: she almost certainly had a tumour. They would wait for confirmation from the biopsy results but it looked like it would need to be removed sooner rather than later.

Back in the waiting room Paula was in tears, while Linda was struggling to come to terms with what had happened that morning. In the space of just two hours her whole world had turned upside down.

Despite the trauma she went back to work that day. It was a brave thing to do. On the surface she carried on as if nothing had changed. But deep down she was in utter turmoil. A week later she was back in hospital for the biopsy results. That waiting period was agony, the worst week of her life. She couldn't sleep and suffered from terrible anxiety. She also developed a terrible cough.

Going to work was the only thing that kept her mind off the tumour, although how she managed to keep going with hardly any sleep for days on end was amazing – especially since we also had three teenage children to look after.

The biopsy confirmed there was a tumour in her breast. But that wasn't the only terrible news for Linda at that point in her life. She'd not long since learned her dad, Frank, was suffering from bowel cancer. So she was forced to keep this terrible news from her parents. She wanted to unburden herself to her mum, Geraldine, but couldn't.

Geraldine was already deeply affected by Frank's poor condition. By now Frank was very ill. He never made it and we both still miss him.

On 2nd June Linda was taken in for the operation to remove the tumour. It was only once proceedings were under way that Geraldine was told what was going on. Linda then underwent a course of radiotherapy, every day for a month at The Beatson Institute in Bearsden from that September.

By coincidence, every Wednesday Linda and her dad were treated at the same time. She got radiotherapy and on the floor above he received chemotherapy. Frank was unaware his daughter was in the same building. Linda kept her dad in the dark because she knew he had enough problems of his own. He found out one day, though, when Geraldine blurted it out. The effect on him was traumatic, but Linda was able to reassure him her condition was improving.

A month later Frank died.

Then, just before Christmas 2011, Linda got the all-clear and went back to work full time. Since then, thankfully, she has been a picture of health. But our troubles weren't over.

Not by a long chalk.

I Belong to Glasgow

WHEN I LOOK BACK and reflect on my life, I can't believe that despite all the setbacks, disappointments and complications I am still here facing my demons with confidence and even aggression. Nothing has come easy to me.

The first serious setback as an adult occurred after the first big pro fight of my career. I had won my first nine bouts and afterwards my dressing room was always mobbed by friends, family and fans. The noisy celebrations would go on and on and although it would be a struggle to find a bit of personal space, it was a fun place to be. But the loser's changing room is a very dark and lonely place.

In the aftermath of my tenth bout, on Tuesday 24th June 1986, I found myself sitting in my own personal morgue in Glasgow's Plaza Ballroom, with tears of despair streaming down my face. I had just gone through the stiffest test of my short career. Only 13 months after my professional debut I had taken on the vastly more experienced Dave Douglas for the vacant Scottish Welterweight title. Just to get this opportunity I needed to overcome what most observers believed was a formidable hurdle.

Glaswegian Billy Cairns was 21st on the UK light-welterweight rankings and I knew him really well. We'd trained in the same gyms and we had sparred from time to time so there should have been no surprises for him, but when it was announced we'd face each other in the final eliminator for the Scottish Welterweight title, what had been a fairly easy-going relationship between us immediately turned sour.

He suddenly began attacking me with verbal insults, belittling my chances predicting that he was going to knock me out. This was no publicity stunt to boost ticket sales because I didn't rise to the bait. It was a serious attempt to goad me and undermine my confidence.

I took little notice of it. I would do all my talking in the ring, and I got my chance to have my say on 14 April 1986, at the Plaza. We were both unbeaten and the victor would go forward to take on former champ Douglas for the vacant title. For the loser obscurity beckoned.

I heard talk beforehand that we were pretty evenly matched and the fight could go either way but in the end I was all over him and beat him on points fairly easily. I had him down twice and I just kept going forward. Cairns tried his best but it wasn't good enough and he couldn't stop me getting through with punches to the head.

That defeat was the beginning of the end for my opponent who had entered the ring having won his first five professional fights. He retired 18 months later at the relatively tender age of 23 with a record of just six wins and three losses. Many boxers didn't stay in the game after losing to me in those days: John Conlan lasted just over a year, Nigel Burke never fought again, Albert Buchanan quit within nine months, as did Courtney Phillips and Alistair Laurie. Tyrell Wilson kept going for 11 months.

There was a good reason for that. The general feeling back then was that Maurice Lewis, my manager and trainer, didn't have a clue about boxing and I just wasn't very good. So those who lost to me must have come to the conclusion that if they couldn't beat me they weren't good enough to make it as a pro. They became disillusioned and quit.

Maurice summed up the situation quite well: "For a long time the only people who took any notice of Gary were those who'd been hit by him. People who watch from ringside are always convinced they can beat him. He's a nice guy outside the ring but his approach to his work is ruthless."

Many of my opponents at that time would have been lulled

into a false sense of security by my short and unremarkable amateur career, but they overlooked the fact that most of my pro fights had gone the distance and, consequently, I was picking up great experience along the way. Those who watched me closely would realise I was getting better and stronger with every fight.

And so it proved against Douglas. I had destroyed him in a monumental battle for the vacant title and should have been shedding tears of joy. Yet, at the end of a mostly one-sided affair, the ref inexplicably raised my opponent's arm.

Douglas, whose father Charlie was the king of Scotland's gypsies, had been Scottish welterweight champion for three-and-a-half years from 1980-84. He'd been around the block a few times and had 39 fights under his belt. Although not in possession of a killer punch, he had a fast jab. He was ring-wise and wily. He knew how to stay out of trouble and tie up his opponents to prevent them from landing the knock-out blows.

He was often lined up as cannon fodder on promotions south of the border, but would frequently surprise so-called superior opponents, who'd been told to expect an easy victory, with his ring craft and cunning. He had a fair number of losses on his record but some of them were in England; tight affairs awarded against him by a home-town ref. On his own turf he might have won most of them. Such is the nature of pro boxing at the lower levels.

As part of his training for the fight against me, Douglas sparred constantly against a couple of useful southpaws so he could familiarise himself with my awkward stance. Although by comparison a novice, most experts had me as a clear favourite to win. They predicted the combination of strength, courage and youth – there was a near ten-year age gap between us – would hand me a clear advantage, and my confidence was boosted by the publication of the official rankings less than three weeks before the fight. In just 11 months I had raced 65 places up the charts and was now 15th in Britain. That made me the highest-ranked Scottish fighter in the welterweight division, two places above Douglas. I always looked out for the rankings. It was really important for me to see my name in the press. It was all part of boosting my reputation and raising my profile.

As the bell rang for the first round on that fateful night, it became abundantly clear the pre-match pundits were bang on, as I quickly floored Douglas for a count of nine with a powerful barrage to the body. Only the bell saved the Larkhall man from a sensational and ignominious early exit. In the second round I continued my all-out assault and a bewildered Douglas found himself stunned again, this time for a count of six.

By now I was in full flow and it looked as though I could end the fight in the third. But Douglas managed to stay on his feet. In the fourth Douglas took another count, as I turned the screw, oozing power with every punch. My opponent, battered and bruised, managed to hang in there for the rest of the fight, jabbing away without inflicting any damage on me. No matter what he did I had an answer. There was nothing he could do to hurt me, but it must have been a painful, forlorn hope for him after such a disastrous start.

At the end of ten rounds few in the Plaza crowd could have denied me a clear victory. I never once stopped going forward, chasing the veteran around the ring and keeping him on the back foot with a fierce display of heavy body shots, but referee Billy Rafferty awarded the title to Douglas. It was an astonishing decision.

Incredibly, I had lost the fight and my unbeaten record. My camp and the majority in the crowd were incensed. Back in the dressing room I was inconsolable. In the ring I had taken and dished out a whole lot of physical pain, but in those days underneath the tough guy image lay a very emotional young man. And the events of that night proved too much for me.

For the one and only time in my career I broke down and cried.

After a fight I could be in my changing room for anything between one and two hours. The adrenalin was still pumping through my body long after the final bell. It would take a while to calm down and get ready to leave.

In the minutes immediately following the Douglas debacle my manager Maurice Lewis and I were alone together. Those who knew us realised it was best not to intrude. It was a silent place with gloom hanging in the air.

Tears began to drip from my eyes. Within a short time I was bawling like a baby and I didn't care who saw it. If I had lost to a superior opponent I would have coped better with defeat. But in my view I had won that fight. And when the decision went against me I just couldn't handle it.

Nothing I'd experienced in life thus far had left me feeling more upset. As a boxer I had two distinct personalities. In the ring I aspired to be the ultimate fighting machine; battling through pain and, at times, injury to win the war. At all other times I was an ordinary man with normal everyday feelings and those feelings were badly hurt.

Most visitors to the changing room that night were quietly shooed away by Maurice. I eventually composed myself and went home. In the solitude of my own bedroom I started sobbing again.

The following day, June 25th, 1986, Maurice fired off a letter the British Boxing Board of Control demanding a re-match. It was written in his usual understated way: "I wish to put forward my boxer Gary Jacobs to challenge for the Scottish Welterweight Title. I feel this is merited due to the controversial outcome of their contest when he boxed Dave Douglas at the Plaza Ballroom."

For me it was back to the drawing board.

As an amateur I had not been too bothered by defeat. I lost four of my 14 fights. But this was different. This was my livelihood.

Maurice realised it would be vital for me to win my next fight. He knew I was deeply upset by the Douglas decision and he didn't want me to wallow in the doldrums too long, in case I started brooding about it. We both knew I had to get the defeat out of my system, and fast. The next fight had to be a confidence booster.

But before that, Maurice decided a holiday in the sun wouldn't do me any harm and so I headed to Tenerife for a week with my pals. It was an off-the-cuff decision which turned out to have far-reaching implications for my career.

I arrived in Santa Cruz, in the northern part of the island, with a couple of pals during the second week of July. We chose that area because it was mildly cooler than the busier southern resorts like Playa de Las Americas. As soon as we touched down it became apparent that almost everyone was talking about nothing other than boxing. In my own naive way I initially wondered if news of my controversial fight with Dave Douglas had reached these shores, but I soon had my card marked by the hotel barman.

It turned out there was a great buzz surrounding a local heavyweight, Jose Antonio Castro, who went by the alias of Toyi. Not surprisingly none of us had heard of him, because he was relatively unknown outside Tenerife and the rest of the Canary Islands. Despite that, Toyi would soon become an inspiration to me. He'd won 11 and lost just once in his short career so far and was entering the ring again in a couple of days' time, in Santa Cruz.

Toyi was unique among professional boxers because he was plying his trade while serving a 16-year jail sentence. A generous prison governor allowed him out to train and fight, but immediately after the bout he went back to his cramped cell. A local boy, the sixth of seven children whose father died when he was 10, Toyi had endured a tough start in life, but he trained as a mechanic and got a decent job on the island.

He was sporty and enjoyed football and boxing in his spare time. Things were looking good for him but in 1977 he got involved in petty crime and was jailed for theft. After his release he continued to fall foul of the law and was sentenced again. In 1979, although in and out of jail, he was considered good enough to represent Tenerife in the Spanish Amateur Championships. He only had 10 fights under his belt but got to the semi-finals.

However, by the end of that year he had been found guilty of two more robberies and of receiving stolen goods. Incredibly, he was sentenced to 30 years, even though no weapons or violence were used in any of the crimes. On appeal, this extremely harsh sentence was reduced to 16 years, which by UK standards still sounds crazy.

Four years later he was transferred to an open prison in return for good behaviour and here he was allowed to resume his boxing training. Through time he was permitted to leave prison on a temporary basis and return to amateur boxing.

It was a tough regime but Toyi gradually overcame hurdles which would have stopped many a lesser man and in 1984 became Spanish Heavyweight Champion. He applied to turn pro shortly after and when his licence came through he was snapped up by Enrique Soria, Spain's top boxing manager at the time.

He won his first 10 pro fights, before he was knocked out in the 11th by American Melvin Epps, then won the 12th. We arrived in Santa Cruz just as Toyi was about to enter the ring for the re-match against Epps and this time the Spaniard avenged his sole defeat to date by winning on points.

When I heard his story, I realised how fortunate I was. It made me realise that it was time to man up and stop feeling sorry for myself.

Toyi was a criminal and he got caught. He was punished, some would say, including me, very harshly. And yet here he was, thankful for the privilege of getting into the ring. It was a privilege I had been taking for granted. I resolved to be more humble and keep my emotions in check when things didn't go my way. I vowed that, win or lose, my next opponent would take on a different, more mature Gary Jacobs, and so it proved on 15 September at Glasgow's St Andrews Club, where I faced Jeff Connors, who for reasons I never discovered or really cared too much about, preferred to be known as Jeff Decker.

Decker, from Whitley Bay, could be described as "rugged". For a boxer who'd won just seven of his 20 fights this was something of a compliment. The bout was scheduled for eight rounds. It didn't even last three. I was determined to prove I was still a force to be reckoned with and Decker's demolition began immediately.

From the first bell I chased the Englishman round the ring, blitzing him with hooks to the head and body. Decker's defence amounted to a few half-hearted jabs. In the second the pressure paid off when Decker's left eye was cut. It was all over for the Geordie before the end of the next round. By now his left cheekbone had been ripped open by my fists of fury and most observers reckoned it was an act of supreme mercy when the referee stepped in to end the fight.

A month later I was back at the St Andrews; Kelvin Mortimer, my next opponent on the comeback trail, had won his first three fights. Coincidentally, he'd defeated three boxers who'd previously lost to me – Tyrell Wilson, John Conlan and Alistair Laurie - but any similarities between us ended there. His unbeaten run was about to come to a painful end.

Mortimer was rumoured to be a bit of a puncher. But after five of the six scheduled rounds it was my punches which ended the contest, with the referee intervening to spare the bleeding Welshman further torment.

By now the Scottish Area Council of the British Boxing Board of Control had sanctioned the re-match everyone had been waiting for: Jacobs v Douglas II would take place on

Tuesday 27 January 1987 at the Plaza. Like our first clash, it would be a sell-out, with black market tickets in big demand.

This time there would be an added bonus. ITV had recently launched their *Fight Night* series and the TV cameras would be there to record the action. It would be the first Scottish fight for ITV and former world lightweight champion Jim Watt would provide expert analysis. Many boxing fans hoped that this would prevent another contentious refereeing decision.

They couldn't have been more wrong.

For me, inwardly seething since losing to Douglas, this was a chance to put things right. This time I wasn't going to leave anything to chance. I was determined to come away with a clear-cut victory.

I knew Douglas couldn't hurt me. And, after putting him down three times in the first fight, I also knew he couldn't take my punches. I knew I wouldn't lose. But I had to do enough to ensure the referee would have no doubts about it.

At the ends of ten rounds I had accomplished my mission. Referee Len Mullen scored the fight in my favour, and that's when the fireworks started. Because most observers in the Plaza, including the majority of my own fans, reckoned Douglas had won! There was universal outrage at the decision, with boos ringing round the packed hall.

"Boxing's Night of Shame" screamed a headline in one paper as a sports columnist described the verdict as "one of the worst decisions ever".

Nights of shame were becoming quite regular at The Plaza in Glasgow. The night I demolished Billy Cairns on April the 14th, had been marred by disgraceful scenes. A welterweight clash between Tommy Cook from Larkhall and Dundee's Joe McNamee turned nasty in the third round when Cook was disqualified for persistent holding. The 24-year-old attacked Glaswegian referee, Danny McCafferty, who tried his best to calm the boxer down while evading his vicious blows. Cook was fined and suspended *sine die*, while the show's promoter Alex

Morrison was also fined £200 for inappropriate behaviour in connection with another bout that night.

After my "night of shame" Douglas's furious manager sent a letter of protest to the Scottish boxing authorities who promised a full enquiry. They assured all and sundry that referee Mullen would be hauled before them to explain his actions. The Douglas camp demanded a re-match. They were so sure of their man's superiority they tried to schedule it for the following month.

One man who wasn't surprised by the verdict was the new Scottish Welterweight Champion - me. That fight should never have happened in the first place. If the referee in the first fight had come up with the correct decision Douglas might never have got a re-match. In the second fight Douglas didn't do much boxing. He relied on jab and grab. He would come in behind his fast jab, catch me a couple of times then grab on to me, holding my arms to prevent me from punching him. He knew if I hit him cleanly it could be all over for him and he did everything to stop me from boxing.

I kept going forward and although I didn't land any great shots I was still the better fighter. And that's why I won.

Years later Len Mullen would only say: "I made Jacobs a clear winner." Despite that vote of confidence Maurice reckoned this was one of my poorest displays.

And on the basis that I couldn't possibly perform as badly again, we immediately offered Douglas the re-match he wanted. The boxing authorities, in response to the public outcry, ordered me to defend my title against Douglas within 30 days or relinquish it.

With both sides apparently eager and willing, the "Showdown at the Plaza", as it was billed in *The Sunday Post*, was arranged for Tuesday 24 February. In an interview with that paper, I told top sportswriter Barry Douglas: "Although I won, it was the worst fight of my career. I was so confident I thought I only had to turn up to win", and I added ominously, "but I won't make the same mistake twice. I can't wait to get Dave Douglas in the ring again. I've got a point to prove and my pride to restore."

And so the scene was set for the decider. The hall was booked and the tickets printed. A sell-out crowd was guaranteed. ITV couldn't wait to get the cameras rolling at Scottish boxing's greatest grudge match.

But suddenly, out of the blue, Douglas pulled out.

He complained that he'd suffered a heavy bout of 'flu and couldn't fight. Instead he was off to Australia for a five-week holiday after which, as it turned out, he would announce his retirement. Douglas attempted a brief comeback eight months later. But after winning one fight then losing another he called it quits for good.

Dave Douglas is one of the nicest guys I met in boxing (although I didn't appreciate that at the time!) and he was interviewed for this book. Here, for the first time, is his verdict on the two fights:

"I knew how to handle southpaws. I'd beaten every one I'd ever fought except for the first one I'd faced as a pro. So I felt I had nothing to fear from Gary. He was very awkward, but the only reason he put me down three times in the first fight is because he hit me below the belt. I don't know if he did it deliberately, but it was sore! The referee didn't do anything about it, he must have been looking at the lights.

"Because of that I didn't really start boxing till near the end of round four, when I was *compos mentis* again. No question Gary had won the first three rounds. By the end of the sixth I was back in the fight.

"Big Alex Morrison, my manager, was in my corner and going into the last round he told me the fight was level. He said 'win this round and you've retained the title. Don't box, go out there and batter him.' And that's exactly what I did for three minutes.

"In the second fight I won it by a country mile. It was about a year later. I was going to live in Australia but my manager told me there was TV interest and good money on offer so I jumped at the chance.

"By now I was 33 years old and really struggling to make the weight. I really wanted to take on George Gipsy Collins at light middleweight that night. But Alex Morrison said 'if you don't fight Gary Jacobs. TV will pull the plug on the whole deal and you'll lose out on a lot of money'.

"Back then you weighed in at one o'clock on the day of the fight so if I'd been over the ten stone seven limit there was hardly any time to lose the excess. I remember thinking that if I'd been told I'd need to lose even just three or four ounces I would have said 'kiss my ass' and walked away.

"But I trained hard for that fight. My brother Alex, who was in the Marines, worked me mercilessly every day to make sure I was ready. It was really tough going to get to that weight but I made it.

"Up against Gary I expected a hard fight. He was tough, fit, game and very, very awkward. But I handled him so easily it was like a good sparring exercise. And if you watch the tape it wasn't a great fight but there was only one man in it.

"After seven rounds John McDermott in Gary's corner was heard on TV telling him he needed to win the next three rounds big to have a chance. He never won any of them. I had doubts about the referee prior to the fight but Alex Morrison said in the dressing room 'it's live on TV if you win it you'll get it'. Well I won it and I never got it."

While I have a degree of sympathy for Dave now, back then I had no time to worry about his feelings. I was the champion and, having dominated the Scottish welterweight scene, was up to tenth in the UK rankings.

True, both of us were unhappy with the refereeing decisions in the two fights. Sometimes it's hard to take and, as my career flourished, I would be forced to face these issues again. Despite the anger these decisions generate, as a professional I would learn to shrug them aside and carry on regardless.

Thankfully I managed to avoid refereeing of the kind *Boxing News* described as a "shambles" in February 1997. The fight, in Bethnal Green, was between British middleweight Adrian Dodson and Frenchman Rachid Serjane. Dodson landed a low blow early on and in the fifth round did it again. I gather both were unintentional but Serjane was left in agony after the second below-the-belt battering. As he lay on the canvas rolling in agony, the ref had the option of bringing in the ringside doctor to check on the injured Frenchman. He refused to do so and then awarded Dodson the fight after disqualifying Serjane for ungentlemanly conduct when he did not get back to his feet. If that had happened at The Plaza I'm sure there would have been a riot.

All these considerations, however, had no impact on me. I had triumphed and was now also the proud possessor of the Steve Watt Memorial Belt.

Steve had been a highly promising Glaswegian welterweight. In October 1985, in only his eleventh professional fight, he won the Scottish title. In March the following year he died after a Southern Area welterweight clash with Rocky Kelly in Fulham. The fight was stopped in the tenth round. The inquest into his death found he had suffered extensive brain damage. Doctors also discovered that Watt had been suffering from boxing-related brain damage for quite some time and his death was caused by the recurrence of an old injury.

His death meant there was no Scottish champion. The first clash between Douglas and I was for the title Steve Watt had tragically vacated. A new belt in his honour was commissioned, to be presented to the winner. Dave Douglas was the first to wear it. Now it was my turn. I did so with immense pride.

Steve's death led to renewed calls for boxing to be banned on medical grounds. As the debate raged, the tale of little-known Scottish-based boxer Brian McCue reared its ugly head. And once again my regular promoter Alex Morison had a role to play.

Boxing News had originally broken the story at around the time Steve Watt won the Scottish Championship. McCue's camp claimed he had 98 heavyweight contests as an amateur, that he had represented Scotland seven times at international level and had held the Scottish Heavyweight title.

However, an investigation by *Boxing News* suggested these claims were bogus. They said McCue had just 11 amateur fights, with only one of them a victory. They also claimed he had been knocked out eight times, with three of those KOs coming from the fists of Alex Morrison, who, at that time, had been the oldest amateur heavyweight in Britain at the age of 44.

The issue became a live one because McCue collapsed at the weigh-in for the Scottish Amateur Championships and a subsequent examination revealed he was suffering from diabetes. McCue's medical card was, consequently, withdrawn by the Scottish ABA, while the surgeon who examined him advised that McCue should never box again. Despite these medical warnings McCue was later granted a professional licence.

My thoughts were torn between Toyi Castro and Steve Watt. Boxing made the former's life meaningful when without it he could have ended up just another ex-con with no future, and yet the death of Steve Watt hammered home that what happened to him could one day happen to me.

It was too difficult for me to reach a definitive opinion on the pros and cons so I decided to let others decide on the future of the fight game.

In the meantime, my thoughts turned to my own future. Next on the horizon was a crack at the Commonwealth title. That fight would lead to more shameful scenes, this time ignited by the spectre of fascist-inspired antisemitism. but before that hurdle could be overcome, typically, there were more difficulties facing me.

From Doncaster to Las Vegas

AFTER THE HIGH DRAMA of the Douglas title clincher it was back down to earth for a more mundane night's work at the Plaza less than a month later, and it was a certainty that a Gary would win!

My opponent on 23rd February, 1987 was Gary Williams, from Doncaster. The Central Area Champion couldn't put up much of a fight though. He was down three times before being knocked out in the seventh of the scheduled eight-rounder. Things might have been different, though, if Maurice hadn't followed his instincts.

He'd originally arranged for me to take on Wally Swift from Birmingham that night, but then at the last minute changed his mind and wanted to call off the fight. He had a niggling doubt that the man he'd picked to face me was the wrong choice.

Dave McCabe, a terrific prospect from Gartcosh, was on the same bill and he was lined up to fight Williams. In the dressing room just a couple of hours before the night's first bout, Maurice suggested that McCabe and I swap opponents and he agreed. I knew nothing of this at the time. My job was to turn up and fight. I didn't really care who was in the opposite corner. As it turned out Maurice had been right to worry. Swift put McCabe down in the third before losing on points at the end of a bruising eight-rounder.

Just over a month later, on 6th April, I was back at the Plaza where Williams' stable mate Robert Armstrong was waiting for me. Armstrong, allegedly out to avenge the Williams defeat and described in the pre-fight hype as 'hard-hitting', fared little better. Once again it was scheduled for eight rounds, but after I knocked him to the deck almost at will the fight was stopped in the fifth. By then Armstrong had been downed four times. He'd required two counts of eight in the third and counts of eight and seven in the fifth. Most of the damage was done by ferocious body shots but his left eye was also badly hit and had closed when the fight was ended. It may have been a trifle unfair but one ringside fan remarked later that Armstrong had hit the canvas more often than he'd hit me.

At any rate, the boys from Doncaster must have enjoyed being painfully humiliated in Scotland. Either that or it was becoming increasingly difficult for Maurice to find meaningful opposition.

On 19th May, six weeks later, Gary Williams was back for more punishment, this time at the Tryst Sports Centre in Cumbernauld. It may have been a different location but the outcome and the manner in which victory was achieved hadn't altered. The eight-rounder was stopped by the referee in the third.

The Doncaster treble had provided me with three easy paynights. Now it was time to step up a gear. My next fight would be against veteran Tommy McCallum at the St Andrews Sporting Club on 8th June and at stake would be my Scottish crown. The 29-year-old from Edinburgh had won the Scottish title in 1984 but then lost it to the ill-fated Steve Watt. He too had warmed up for the title fight by taking on Gary Williams, but McCallum had looked far from convincing in a points victory.

Veteran coach John McDermott was in my corner that night along with Maurice. He told me later, "As we entered the ring I overheard two fans discussing the outcome and one predicted a McCallum victory because Ken Buchanan was in his corner." Buchanan or not, I wasn't taking any chances. About three weeks before the title defence I'd started training in the Thomas a Beckett gym in London. This legendary gym no longer exists but at the time I went there it was one of the most famous boxing gyms in the world. It was on the first floor of a three-storey building on the Old Kent Road, above a pub with the same name. Over 100 world champions had trained there including Muhammad Ali, Joe Frazier and Sugar Ray Leonard. The late, great Sir Henry Cooper, former British, European and Commonwealth Heavyweight Champion, trained there six days a week for 14 years from 1954 and, in 1984, briefly took over the running of the pub.

For me being there was extra special. Not only was I broadening my boxing horizons by working out with a whole new range of difficult and tricky sparring partners, but I enjoyed soaking up the atmosphere and history of the building. It was a magical place, especially for a music fan like me when I discovered that a small room above the gym was used by David Bowie and the Spiders from Mars for rehearsals. Not only was it the birthplace of so many great boxing careers but also Ziggy Stardust!

Later the gym was managed by an up-and-coming star of British boxing. Dean Powell was just 22 when he took over and a few years down the line he would become my trainer. I travelled back and forth to London several times prior to the McCallum fight. Maurice and I stayed with his cousin Marcus Pogalewitz who had a flat in Ealing Broadway.

Training at the Thomas a Beckett was hard work but it wasn't always serious. I was booked to spar with another young, talented fighter from London who had a big fight coming up against a southpaw. The deal was I would spar with him twice a day for five days. It suited both of us because he had a good reputation.

On the morning of the second day his trainer approached Maurice and asked if I would stop using my right hand while sparring with his boy. Apparently he couldn't cope with it. Maurice and I decided to ignore him and I spent the next four days hitting him as often as possible with my right fist. He never managed to contain that shot and unsurprisingly went on to lose the fight.

Joking apart, I was going from strength to strength. Nine days before facing McCallum I took part in a mile race for boxers in London in aid of charity and won without too much trouble. Taking care of McCallum at Glasgow's Albany Hotel proved to be just as easy. He was regarded as a master tactician but I ripped his pre-fight plan to shreds. I was younger, fitter, hungrier and I took control right from the start, launching powerful hooks to his midriff. The body barrage continued with McCallum appearing to offer no meaningful defence. By the start of the fifth round it was obvious the end was in sight. A right hook put him down for six and at that point I thought he should have stayed down because he was in real pain. But all credit to him he got up and tried to get through the round, no-doubt hoping to catch me with a wild sucker punch, but I wasn't letting him off the hook and I just kept after him. He had nothing left and I knew he couldn't hurt me. McCallum was given two more counts in that round and, after a couple of ferocious shots to the head, found himself on the ropes unable to defend himself before the ref brought a very one-sided bout to an end.

It was a sweet triumph for me. There was no doubt about the result and now nobody could question my right to the Scottish title. It was time for a well-earned break and I headed off to Majorca with some pals, while Maurice remained in Glasgow to plot our next move.

Possibly encouraged by my progress in the Thomas a Beckett, he decided the next fight would be in London. Maurice was pally with London-based promoter Harry Holland who was arranging a British title clash between Rocky Kelly and Kirkland Laing at the Ramada Inn, Fulham in November 1987. Holland agreed to put me on the undercard. As ever, my opponent was carefully selected by Maurice and this time, because it was my London-debut, he was more cautious than normal.

Maurice knew of one boxer who was guaranteed not to

put up much of a fight against me and that was Jeff Connors or Decker. Connors/Decker had been my first opponent as I made my comeback after the shattering defeat to Dave Douglas. He was picked out then because I needed, and got, a morale-boosting easy victory.

That had been just over a year earlier and barring some miraculous improvement in his ability he was just the sort of journeyman who would make me look not just good, but great, in front of a big London crowd.

The first time we met I stopped him in three rounds. This time the man from the North East of England fared rather better and lasted the full eight rounds before losing on points. It was a satisfactory, if not spectacular, performance from me, even though I won every round. Kirkland Laing, meanwhile, retained his British Welterweight title by stopping Rocky Kelly in the fifth.

A few weeks later the British rankings were published and I had climbed up to eighth. Above me were Rocky Kelly and George Collins, two fighters with whom I would soon cross swords. And at number five, just to confirm Maurice's earlier misgivings, was Wally Swift. Strangely, although he'd recently retired, Larkhall's Dave Douglas was still ranked at number ten.

In February 1988, a few weeks after the publication of the rankings, I faced my toughest test to date. This time there was no careful matchmaking. The opponent would be Delroy Bryan, an up-and-coming star, and the fight, at the Scottish Exhibition and Conference Centre in Glasgow, would be an eliminator for the British title. The winner would get a shot at the great Kirkland Laing.

Bryan only had 15 fights under his belt and had lost four of them, which compared poorly with my 17-1 record, but among his notable scalps were Darren Dyer, who'd won Commonwealth gold at Edinburgh in 1986, Mickey Hughes, a hot prospect from London and British Light-Welterweight champ Lloyd Christie.

This more ambitious approach came as a result of the conclusion of a management agreement between Maurice and me. My growing reputation had caught the eye of the top men in British boxing – Mike Barrett and Mickey Duff – and they had invited me to join their stable. Maurice and I had originally signed a three-year contract, which had now come to an end. We both knew that I had gone as far as I could under his guidance and that I would have to base myself in London to further my career. There was no animosity, just a realisation that it was time to move on.

Maurice and I had built up a tremendous bond and that remained unbroken. I knew that I owed him everything and that without him I'd be nothing as a boxer. So when I signed for Barrett and Duff I ensured that no matter who I fought, no matter where in the world, Maurice would still be in my corner.

Although thrilled to be joining such an illustrious organisation, my new contractual arrangement hadn't got off to the best possible start.

The deal came about after a phone call from Mike Barrett who invited Maurice and I down to London. The office he shared with Mickey Duff was huge and I remember bumping into Terry Lawless on the way in. We went for lunch and afterwards I decided to sign with Barrett and Duff, as long as I could keep Maurice, which was agreed.

We went straight back to the office from the restaurant to sort out the paperwork and I signed on the dotted line. I thought I'd hooked up with both Barrett and Duff. But unknown to me they'd fallen out a few days earlier and had gone their separate ways. They were always falling out but always made up. This time, though, the split was final. The upshot was I had signed with Barrett and not Duff. Although disappointed by this unexpected turn of events I was forced to push these thoughts aside and concentrate on my career.

By now Bobby Neill had taken over my training routine. Hailing from Edinburgh, he had held the British Featherweight crown in the 1950s but was forced to retire in November 1960 after a brain injury suffered as a result of a knock-out. He had collapsed in his dressing room after being floored twice and stopped in the 14th round by former Olympic champion Terry Spinks. Bobby had needed an operation to remove a blood clot from his brain. He remained unconscious for three days and spent weeks in hospital.

After making a full recovery, and despite losing some of his memory, he became a boxing manager and was soon regarded as the best in Britain having helped Alan Minter and Lloyd Honeyghan to world titles. Bobby had suffered much more out of the ring than within it, leading to him being described as the Miracle Man of Boxing. By the age of 17 he had become a very promising young amateur. One day as he was cycling home a motorcyclist accidentally skidded into him. He was rushed to hospital where surgeons discovered he'd broken his left thigh bone just above his knee. Repairing the damage was difficult and required the insertion of a metal plate and, to add to his woes, he was forced to wear a plaster on his leg for 18 months and spend all of that time lying on his back. Bobby kept his mind ticking over by reading every boxing book he could get his hands on.

He left hospital on walking sticks, determined to get back to full fitness as soon as possible. Before long he erected a tent in his back garden and started training again on his own. After working on his mobility and boxing technique he was ready to resume his career and turned up at the Sparta Club in Edinburgh and calmly informed everybody he was ready to box again. Initially he wasn't taken seriously but within a short time he began beating opponents.

However the accident had left him with a stiff knee and reduced mobility which restricted his footwork. Despite that, within just 12 months he was the Western District Champion.

When he decided to turn pro he moved to London and started training in the Thomas a Becket. He won his first 15 fights, including the vacant Scottish Featherweight title against Matt Fulton. Two more victories followed before his first defeat to Jimmy Brown in Belfast.

In 1957, having been a pro for two years, he was seriously hurt in a car crash and the resultant surgery meant his left leg shorter than his right and surgeons told him he would never box again. But Bobby was determined to prove them wrong and just nine months later he announced his comeback. In May 1958 he was back in the ring and won his first six comeback fights on the trot. This earned him a shot at the British Featherweight title against Charlie Hill. Incredibly, he won and made two successful defences.

His final fight came in late 1960 when he faced Terry Spinks in a rematch for the British title, which Spinks had taken from him two months earlier. This time there was to be no fairytale ending. Bobby was knocked out and needed a month in hospital to recover. Even he knew there was no way back into the ring and he decided to go into management.

By the time we met he worked in partnership with Barrett and Duff and was full of praise for me after we'd been together for just a short while. In an interview with the *Daily Record*'s Dick Currie in the lead-up to the Bryan fight he said, "I've never had a fighter who has adapted so quickly to my method of training. The reigning British welter champion is Kirkland Laing who trains in our gym. And although Gary has never sparred with him, I know Gary would beat him. I've worked with a lot of good champions but they have never been so keen to learn as Gary."

Mike Barrett was also talking me up. He told John Quinn of the *Evening Times*, "Gary has the skill, ambition and dedication to go all the way to the top. When Bobby and I were discussing his future with him I told Gary I would do my utmost to take him to British, Commonwealth and European championships."

While my new management team were confident of my success, I wasn't so sure. The self-doubt which had dogged my career so far seemed to intensify for a while. When I saw Delroy Bryan enter the ring at the SECC in Glasgow I got really worried. He had an amazing physique. He had muscles on muscles. I reckoned he had muscles growing on his ears and I wondered if I could ever hit him hard enough to hurt him. I was also worried that he was so strong he might seriously hurt me. It took a few quiet words from Maurice and Bobby to reassure me and calm me down.

The fight was scheduled for 10 rounds and went the distance. It was close. Bryan started well, making full use of his superior reach but, perhaps realising that my opponent looked more powerful than he really was, I gained in confidence as the fight progressed and landed several of my trademark body shots to the delight of the big crowd. The turning point came in the seventh. At that stage there was little between us before I struck with a solid right to his chin and from then on I completely dominated proceedings. In the end the referee decided that I had won six rounds, lost two and drawn two. It was another great victory for me and opened the door to a shot at the title, but there was sadness, too.

Top of the bill that night was the British Lightweight title clash between holder Alex Dickson and Steve Boyle. The classy Dickson and I had become good friends. We'd met in London and ended up sharing a flat together in the capital. After I signed for Mike Barrett, I was staying in Swiss Cottage in a flat owned by businessman Ivor Tiefenbrun. Ivor was a pal from Glasgow who wanted to help me and since the flat was empty he offered it to me on a short-term basis free of charge. Alex had also recently signed for Barrett and he, too, was staying and training in London, for the Boyle fight, in a place provided by Barrett.

One day he invited me round to his place after training.

When we got there I couldn't believe my eyes. It was about 16 floors up in a council high-rise on the notorious Broadwater Farm estate. There had been riots there less than three years earlier when a policeman had been hacked to death by a mob. It wasn't exactly the safest place to be. There was no way I was staying there a minute longer than necessary. I felt sorry for Alex and invited him to move in with me, where there was plenty of room. He jumped at the chance and we soon became good mates.

That night I watched from the back of the hall as the classy Dickson began stamping his superiority over Boyle. I was chatting with a journalist friend when, suddenly, in the second round, the challenger threw a massive punch which connected perfectly with Dickson's face and knocked him out. Like everyone else in the arena, I was stunned. My pal was taken to hospital where he needed stitches to repair a gash in his cheek. He was okay but it spelled the beginning of the end for his career.

Yet while Alex was struggling, I was going from strength to strength. Less than two weeks later it was announced that I'd take on Commonwealth champion Wilf Gentzen from Australia at Glasgow's Kelvin Hall in the middle of April 1988. The fight was just seven weeks away.

However, controversy erupted over the deal almost immediately. A day earlier Frank Warren had announced that Gentzen had agreed to meet his fighter, George Collins, in London on 29th March. As a bitter war of words escalated Warren claimed, "I have an agreement with Gentzen's agent, Cos Sita, who holds the promotional rights, and it's signed by the boxer himself. As far as I am concerned I have the fight and if anybody says it can't go ahead, I will issue an injunction. My agreement is legal and binding."

A furious Mike Barrett responded by flying to Glasgow where, brandishing several sheets of paper, he announced, "There is absolutely no truth in reports that Gentzen will defend his title in England. He meets Gary Jacobs, we are paying him £10,000 and I have the signed contract here to prove it."

The British Boxing Board of Control were called in to adjudicate. Their secretary, John Maurice, issued the following statement, "Mr Barrett has lodged the contracts for the fight signed by Gentzen and his father, who also acts as his manager. Mr Warren has lodged a contract signed only by an agent in Australia. It is for the Title Committee to decide." Unsurprisingly, given the evidence, Barrett got the vote and I got my crack at the Commonwealth title. However that short-lived rumpus was small beer compared to the storm generated when Gentzen arrived in Glasgow.

In the lead up to the fight Mike Barrett continued to heap praise on me and, at the same time, provided an insight into the way my mind was working. "Gary Jacobs is exceptionally talented, a nice boxer and one of the fastest learners I've seen. I'm delighted to have him. He's ambitious and has set his sights on winning a world title. That's a long way off yet but he's improving all the time. We do have to work on improving his punching power, for Gary is more of a boxer than a scrapper, but this is mainly a matter of balance. The potential is there."

Wilf Gentzen flew into Glasgow on 12th April 1988, exactly a week before the showdown. Apart from the minor inconvenience of becoming the first foreign boxer to undergo a mandatory AIDS test in Scotland, there was nothing to suggest that a huge row was about to erupt. He and I were extremely polite to each other and appeared to be more interested in behaving with dignity rather than putting on the stereotypical snarling, eye-balling, 'I hate you, let's try and sell more tickets' act – but it proved to be the calm before the storm.

Gentzen's credentials as a champion were undisputed. The 25-year-old had lost just two of his 17 fights, both to WBC Super Lightweight champ Tony Jones. As an amateur he had toured England, Ireland and Wales with a team of 15 Aussie fighters and was the only one to return home unbeaten. As a pro he'd spent time in Detroit where he trained in the world famous Kronk Gym alongside Tommy Hearns. His nickname was "White Lightning". His father Dick, who was also his manager, explained it was because he had fast hands. He was clean-cut and tanned and spoke respectfully about me saying, "I have seen him in action only on film, just for a couple of rounds, but I know he is very capable and I'm sure it will be a good, tough 12-round fight next week. There will be no excuse from me about jet lag or anything. I'll be well accustomed to the conditions come fight night."

I responded equally eloquently. "I don't know much about the champion but I have a lot of respect for him and will continue to do so until the first bell goes." It was a surreal build-up to a title fight and the phoney peace couldn't last. When it eventually ended there were unfortunate consequences, the memory of which continue to linger.

Peter McLean, who went on to find fame as head of PR at Celtic FC during the Fergus McCann revolution was, at that time, in charge of sports promotion at Glasgow City Council. He was, and still is, a friend of mine. The city was trying to market itself as an international boxing venue and Peter's department were involved in promoting the Commonwealth title bash. He recalled, "Gentzen's dad was asked by a reporter if he'd ever been to Scotland. He replied, 'just once. I was in the Luftwaffe and we were bombing Clydebank'."

That casual remark brought a serious edge to what had thus far been a tame build up, suddenly there was real tension in the air. Dick Gentzen then fuelled the fire by insisting that a non-Jewish referee should be appointed. Gentzen was under the misapprehension that Mickey Vann was Jewish!

I, wisely, recognised those comments as an attempt to unsettle me. But although I didn't rise to the bait, my public statements took on a more confrontational style. I was angry but I didn't want Gentzen to realise it. I told one reporter, "I'm going to stop him. I've got my mind on bigger things. I know nothing about Gentzen. I don't bother about that. I let him worry about me." To another I said, "He will be just a stepping stone on my way to the world title."

Wilf was becoming embarrassed by his father's anti-Semitic outbursts and at one point pointedly told him to "shut the fuck up".

There was, however, a far more sinister outcome to the war of words, as Peter McLean recalls. "It generated a supposedly Nazi link to a fight involving a Jewish boxer. I was at the fight and unfortunately a group of British National Party activists had turned up and were shouting all sorts of anti-Semitic insults at Gary. I remember feeling absolutely disgusted by their behaviour. There were about 15 or 20 of them and they'd gone to the trouble of buying tickets just to abuse Gary. You could hear their racist, antisemitic chants quite clearly. It was appalling." I had been fighting with a Star of David on my shorts since turning pro and I couldn't care less about the Nazis. I would respond to them my way, in the ring with my fists.

From the first bell I took the fight to the Australian and by the end of that opening round the champ's left eye was cut. As the fight progressed I maintained my onslaught and ignited the 2000-plus crowd by landing vicious left hooks which left my opponent badly shaken. It was the seventh round before Gentzen began showing his worth and he also enjoyed a good eighth round, but by then it was far too late. In any event I upped my pace and in the ninth a vicious left from me almost put the Aussie on his back. By the end of 12 rounds the identity of the winner was beyond doubt. I had fought the fight of my life.

London ref Mickey Vann scored the contest 118.5-117 in my favour. That meant I had won six rounds, drawn three and lost three. Most commentators felt Vann was being unduly generous to Gentzen. In fact Dick Currie of the *Daily Record*, a former Scottish Flyweight champ before becoming a highly-respected sportswriter, reckoned I had won 10 rounds, drawn one and lost just one.

It didn't matter. It had been a comprehensive victory and now, at just 22, I was the new Commonwealth Welterweight Champion. This was my 19th victory in 20 fights and I was quick to thank Mike Barrett and Bobby Neill for the way they prepared me. Their professional influence had certainly rubbed off on me.

Before I got down to my final preparations for this fight, I had spent three weeks at a special fitness centre in London's Covent Garden. There was no boxing involved, mostly circuit training and endurance work. When I'd finished there I felt fitter than ever. Apparently Mike Tyson followed this routine before he fought and it certainly paid off for him. I also tried to change my whole mental approach for this fight. Before some of my earlier bouts I would have let things people have said or done get to me. This time I was able to shut all the distractions out of my mind. Nothing interfered with my preparations, not even Gentzen senior's attempt to unsettle me before the fight.

With my new title came new fame. Suddenly I was in demand. When Celtic skipper Paul McStay was voted Scotland's player of the month for March, I was asked to present the award. This was the start of a great deal of newspaper interest in Scotland's newest champ and I was soon in the spotlight again.

Throughout my short career I'd been compared favourably with Vic Herman, the last Scottish-based Jewish boxer to hold a title. Born in Manchester, Vic grew up in Glasgow, which became his home town. He was an exciting flyweight and Scottish champion in the 1950s. He failed to win the British title but at one point was ranked number two in the world by *Ring* Magazine. Apart from being an accomplished boxer, Herman was a bagpipe-playing virtuoso. When he retired from the ring he turned to another form of canvas and became a highly-respected artist whose paintings could be found at exhibitions around the world.

A few weeks after winning the Commonwealth belt I met him. Herman now lived in the USA and was visiting Glasgow with his son, Maurice, a film director who was making a movie about his father's upbringing in the Gorbals. I told the press, "Vic was my inspiration when I started boxing. I can't believe I've actually met him." Herman responded with equal grace: "I'm really happy that a young Jewish kid such as Gary has come along to take my place in boxing here in Glasgow. The fight fans here are the best. They were good to me and I'm sure Gary will get the same support."

Mike Barrett, meanwhile, was injecting a slight note of caution to the after-match euphoria when he said, "Here we have an exciting fighter. However, the lad is only 22 and still learning his trade. I reckon we can get him a British title fight against Kirkland Laing in the autumn. But I would hope he would have at least two more fights before then. There is no way I would rush a potentially good fighter. Gary is 200 per cent better than when he beat Del Bryan two months ago, but talk of world challenges is, at this juncture, premature."

To prove the point, for my next fight Barrett selected a durable opponent, who might test me but not beat me. Mexican Juan Alonzo Villa was described as tough, hard-hitting and someone I could learn from. In announcing the match-up at a charity show scheduled for London's Hilton Hotel on 6th June, Barrett said, "The British Boxing Board of Control want Gary to meet Kirkland Laing for the British title but despite the fact he has earned this I feel it will be a stupid fight for Gary at the moment. I have informed the Board that Gary will be prepared to meet Laing at the end of this year or early in 1989 but most certainly not right now.

"Kirkland Laing is a highly capable fighter who is rated sixth in the world by *Boxing News*. Gary is not yet in this league but I am confident he can get there eventually. Laing proved in beating Roberto Duran that he can take care of himself in any company. He is the type of fighter who can make even the best look sluggish and amateurish.

"Before Gary goes in with him, if ever at all, he will need more experience and that is what we are aiming for right now. And only after several more similar ventures will we even think of Laing. Gary would take on anyone so it is vital that those of us in charge of his career should ensure he is carefully looked after. Only when we feel he is ready will we let him go all out, but by then he will be really worth watching."

I knew my manager was talking sense and that I needed another good performance because it was crucial to impress London fight fans. At that stage of my career it was still definitely a case of 'Gary who?' in the capital.

On the night, Villa's hopes were quickly reduced to rubble. He had entered the ring with 16 wins and eight losses and after five fairly one-sided rounds the referee decided he'd seen enough and stopped the contest to save the Mexican further torture. He'd taken several big shots to the head and was badly cut. One commentator was heard to remark, "not so much Pancho Villa (referring to the legendary Mexican general), more punchless Villa."

The victory seemed to snap Mike Barrett out of his usual restrained approach. "The way he has been advancing makes me believe he will win the world title in two years' time." It was a bold prediction but Barrett had a couple of more gems up his sleeve. He confirmed he'd been working to line up a big TV fight with an as yet unnamed opponent in Las Vegas and revealed, "I'm involved now with other boxing people in a TV cable network to stage regular boxing there and all my fighters will be involved."

Barrett's Vegas deal was sealed at a secret meeting with one of the Mr Bigs of American boxing, Bob Arum. The pair had got together in the unlikely setting of San Remo in Italy to discuss ways of making me a worldwide household name. Their plan was to arrange fights for me in Vegas and Atlantic City, followed by a few more in the UK. Their ultimate aim was to get me a crack at the world title within two years.

Then Barrett dropped another bombshell when he announced I would defend my Commonwealth title in Israel! He explained, "I'm forming an alliance with an American millionaire called Aaron Bronstein who is a fight enthusiast. There hasn't been any professional boxing in Israel but I'm sure there is a huge market for it and Gary is capable of emulating great Jewish fighters we have had like Ted 'Kid' Lewis and Jackie 'Kid' Berg. The Israelis are crying out for a top-class professional show and Gary is top of their list because he is Jewish."

I thought this was great news. "It's too marvellous for words," I told a reporter. "I have always wanted to fight in Las Vegas and being Jewish, to box in Israel is a dream come true."

A few months later the Las Vegas fight appeared to be taking shape. Caesar's Palace Pavilion was by now the agreed venue and TV coverage was confirmed by ESPN. Talk of a Commonwealth title defence in Tel Aviv, however, had all but dried up. By mid-August I learned I'd face a severe test in Vegas. My opponent, Javier Suazo, was ranked 14th in the world, three places above me, and great things were expected of him. Nine months earlier he'd gone the distance with former WBA World Welterweight champ Mark Breland. He'd lost on a unanimous decision but had not been disgraced.

The pair of us would battle it out on 16th September 1988 over 12 rounds for the vacant WBC International Welterweight crown, which is a title available to boxers ranked 10th to 30th in the world. For me the stakes were massive. A good win could make me an overnight star in America. A loss would probably spell the end my dream over there. You don't get too many second chances in America.

To prepare for the biggest test of my career I, accompanied by my pal Alex Dickson, headed off to the English West Country where I would endure two of the toughest weeks of my life. Alex and I went through a punishing training routine set up by fitness experts at the University of Bath. Mike Barrett described it as a 'torture chamber' and he was right. I endured a strict 11-hour daily regime of running, swimming, weight training and circuit work. These were the most intensive preparations I had ever gone through for a fight and it showed how seriously we rated the threat from Suazo.

In public, Mike Barrett appeared quite relaxed about the showdown. "Jacobs is now stepping into the big time and the opportunities America presents are fantastic. We think of him as a future world champion. Suazo is a good fighter with fast hands but I wouldn't let Gary anywhere near him if I didn't think he could take him," he said.

So far, Barrett's handling of my career had been outstanding. His shrewd manoeuvring of a relatively unknown young Scot, who hadn't even fought for the British title, into the American TV spotlight showed why he had become such a household name in world boxing. And, as it transpired, his judgement of Suazo was spot on.

The fight was scheduled for 12 rounds and the first three were fairly even. But after that I didn't lose a round and my punches were wearing him down. In the tenth I caught him with a load of hard body shots. He went down and couldn't get up. It was the best fight of my life.

At the time I just could not have been happier. I felt so delighted and so proud to win this title. I was now the WBC International World Welterweight Champion and, more importantly, an overnight sensation as far as millions of American TV fans were concerned.

Mike Barrett, the great promoter that he was, was milking my performance for all it was worth. He said, "Gary received such applause from the 4500 crowd you would not believe.

If he wanted to live here in Las Vegas they would be over the moon. I've had calls from everywhere in America telling me what a helluva fighter he is and the Americans want him back. Gary is the finest prospect I've seen in years and I'm convinced he will be world champion within 12 months. He will need around seven or eight fights before we consider the world title, but he is a world champion in the making, make no mistake about that."

While it was an important and exciting night for me, the gamble in Vegas paid off in more ways than one. A couple of days before the fight I had taken a break from training and was lounging by the Caesar's Palace pool when another hotel guest approached me. It was a chance encounter that would change my life. This wee old guy came up to me and asked if I was Gary Jacobs. He then introduced himself as Bobby Sulkin and told me he was a big fan.

"Do you know my boys?" he asked. "They're well-known in London and love their boxing." I'd never heard of them so Bobby invited me to his room from where he phoned his sons, Graham and Gary.

We started chatting and they told me that when I got back to London they would take me out and show me a good time. I'd been in London for most of that year and had kept myself to myself. I didn't have any close pals down there and didn't socialise much, I just worked away every day training all the time. I was happy with that monastic lifestyle but the prospect of getting out and letting my hair down from time to time was intriguing. In any event, there was something about Bobby that I really liked and I knew I'd made a new friend.

After the fight I went on a well-earned week's holiday to California. When I arrived back in London I phoned Graham who told me Bobby was in hospital. It was the day I arrived back and Graham picked me up at my flat and took me to see his dad, who needed a bypass. I walked into his room and he was in bed. When he saw me he jumped out. He was wearing a dressing gown with 'Bobby Sulkin World Champ' on the back! Bobby survived his operation and I went on to form a deep and lasting friendship with the Sulkin family.

There was a fascinating footnote to my night in Vegas. On the undercard there was a very one-sided Bantamweight contest between Johnny Tapia and Miguel Martinez, which Tapia won with a first-round KO. Tapia's life story is perhaps one of the most tragic in modern boxing. And yet it illustrated once again how the sport can make a positive impact on even the worst-case scenario, if only for a short while.

Johnny Tapia was described by Mike Tyson as one of the greatest fighters ever. He died at the tender age of 45 but, by all accounts, he wouldn't have lasted anywhere near that long without boxing. Born in the rough South Side of Albuquerque, New Mexico on Friday, 13th February 1967. it was believed that Johnny's father had been murdered while he was still in his mother's womb.

When he was eight years old, Johnny witnessed his mother being kidnapped. She was later raped, repeatedly stabbed, and murdered by her assailant. She was just 33 years of age and police said she had been stabbed 22 times with an ice pick and left to die on the side of the road. Johnny heard her screaming as she was driven away, chained to the back of a pickup truck, but no-one came to the rescue as the little boy cried for help.

The orphan was taken in by his grandparents and he was taught to fight by his grandfather, an amateur boxing champion. Johnny later recalled that his uncles were betting on his early fights and if he lost they assaulted him. He grew up to become an exceptional streetfighter but hung out with local gangs and was sucked into a near lifelong dependence on cocaine and alcohol.

He was declared clinically dead four times as a result of drug overdoses and he attempted suicide several times as he struggled with manic depression and Post Traumatic Stress

Disorder. On his wedding night, his new wife, Teresa, found him overdosed in the bathroom, a needle in his arm. On another occasion he was in hospital in a coma, receiving treatment for a cocaine overdose, and his brother-in-law and nephew were killed in a car accident on their way to visit him. He was in and out of jail and rehab, which kept him out of the ring for seven years. Despite all these unimaginable handicaps he was a five-time world champion at three different weights.

As his career blossomed Teresa insisted his mother's murder case should be re-opened and DNA evidence finally found the culprit, the last man to have been seen with her. Sadly, there was no opportunity for justice because the murderer had died eight years earlier after stumbling drunk into a busy Albuquerque street, where he was hit by three cars and dragged to his death.

In 2010, at the age of 43, Johnny discovered that his father, Jerry Padilla, had been alive all along. He reappeared in Johnny's life after being released from prison, with a DNA test confirming the relationship. In another poignant twist it transpired the men had known each other for quite some time.

On 27th May 2013, Johnny was found dead inside his Albuquerque home. The cause of death was recorded as heart failure and the onset of Hepatitis C, possibly from the many tattoos he had. His wife Teresa held a press conference to dispel the myth that he had died due to a drugs overdose. She said her husband was taking medication for his bipolar disorder and for his high blood pressure at the time of his death.

At the beginning of his 2006 autobiography, *Mi Vida Loca: The Crazy Life of Johnny Tapia*, he wrote: "My name is Johnny Lee Tapia. I was born on Friday the 13th. A Friday in February of 1967. To this day I don't know if that makes me lucky or unlucky. When I was eight I saw my mother murdered. I never knew my father. He was murdered before I was born.

"I was raised as a pit bull. Raised to fight to the death.

Four times I was declared dead. Four times they wanted to pull life support. And many more times I came close to dying. But I have lived and had it all. I have been wealthy and lost it all. I have been famous and infamous. Five times I was world champion.

"You tell me. Am I lucky or unlucky?"

As Seen on TV

MIKE BARRETT AND I were enjoying a great partnership. Although we didn't have a close personal bond, our professional relationship was very good and, in the short term, would continue to improve. But it wouldn't be long before cracks would begin to appear. Tension and ill-will would take over. The cracks would become chasms.

For now, as we both basked in the after-glow generated by the triumph over Suazo, everything in our garden was rosy. Even before the Suazo fight Barrett had been planning ahead. Within days of the Vegas victory he was announcing that I would soon make a voluntary defence of my Commonwealth title in Glasgow against Zimbabwe's Richard Rova. A few weeks later the date was confirmed, 29th November, but, to my great disappointment, the venue had been altered from the Kelvin Hall to the Royal Albert Hall.

Mike Barrett was also disappointed, for different reasons. In an interview he hit out at the UK's television bosses for their lack of interest in me. The stunning victory over Suazo wasn't picked up by any British network, even though I was massive on American TV. Now the same powerful media moguls were showing little interest in my Commonwealth defence.

"Why don't they wake up to the fact he is one of the hottest prospects for years," fumed Barrett, "It's frustrating when you think that over here they pay out a lot of money on mugs. Stiffs are brought in time and time again to build up so-called British prospects. When the real test comes they're found out, they can't fight. But this guy of mine can."

Despite this apparent setback, Barrett was confident he would fix me up with a crack at one of the three world titles within the next 12 months. The holders at that point were Lloyd Honeyghan (WBC), Colombian Thomas Molinares (WBA) and American Simon Brown (IBF). The last-named would play a significant role in my career, even though we would never fight one another. We were, however, listed to face each other as part of Barrett's masterplan.

At one point he was confident I would fight Brown in Glasgow for the IBF world title by June 1989, just seven months away. He said, "It will take place on a Saturday night and will be broadcast live on TV in America. Home Box Office, the big US cable network, has almost finalised plans for a series of unification fights involving the champions from the three boxing bodies.

"First up, at Caesar's Palace, Las Vegas, in February they're planning a massive double-header. Lloyd Honeyghan will defend his WBC belt against Marlon Starling. The same bill will include Thomas Molinares from Colombia against Mark Breland for the WBA crown. The winners will clash in April and the winner of that fight will take on the IBF champion later in the year, and I hope Gary will be representing the IBF."

The lack of TV coverage in the UK was grating on me. As I prepared to return to Bath University for more specialised conditioning training with athletics coach Tom Hudson as part of my pre-fight build-up, I told reporters, "Tom's contribution has nothing to do with boxing technique but concentrates on weights, running and improving my cardiovascular system. It is all designed to put something extra in my tank and I have found that in my last two title fights I was able to punch harder and faster than the other two men. It is a method of training used by Russian boxers. My only regret is that neither of my fights against Gentzen or Suazo were seen on TV here so the difference it has made to me could have been noticed and appreciated."

As the fight with Rova grew nearer both Bobby Neill and

Mike Barrett were promoting my claims to a world title fight. Lloyd Honeyghan and Simon Brown were touted as possible opponents in open discussions which appeared to indicate the Zimbabwean was beaten long before he even set foot in the ring. Barrett, in what could be described as a potentially negative influence on ticket sales, said he didn't expect the top-of-the-bill bout to last more than four rounds.

I underlined the confidence felt by our camp when I added at a press conference, "I think I'm the greatest thing. I'm very quick, I don't take a lot of punches, I don't smoke, I don't drink and I don't have doubts."

Richard Rova must have been listening too intently to the pre-fight predictions because his challenge was indeed all over in the fourth round. The 30-year-old was highly experienced with 44 fights under his belt, although he'd lost almost as many as he'd won. However, it's unlikely he'd ever faced such a hard hitter because my fierce body shots were too much for him. When the bell went for the fourth round, Rova was lucky to still be on his feet, such was the level of punishment he had been forced to endure. Just over a minute later it was all over. The plucky challenger was pinned down in his own corner attempting to shield himself from a barrage of shots to the head and body. Then I connected with a devastating left hook to the chin. Rova went down and was counted out.

Afterwards Jack 'Kid' Berg, the former Jewish World Junior Welterweight champion, who was by then 80, came into to the ring to congratulate me with a hug, Maurice Lewis turned to me and said, "As far as title defences go, that was your Christmas present. From now on they'll be much tougher." And Kid Berg had a few words of wisdom for 'Kid' Jacobs. The Whitechapel Whirlwind had been the last British Jewish fighter to win a world title. He said, "I like Gary's style but I'm afraid if he keeps holding his right hand so low he will get knocked out himself," and, in a dig at Rova, he added, "but I must say in my day my opponent used to hit me back."

All joking aside, the Rova fight was the most dangerous of my career. As part of the build-up, Mike Barrett and Bobby Neil arranged for me to spar with heavier boxers. Finding sparring partners at my weight had always been a problem, even back in the early days in Glasgow with Maurice Lewis. I was such a hard puncher that few fighters wanted to go into the ring with me. Consequently, Maurice had to bring them up from south of the border. They'd arrive, two or three at a time, and stay with Maurice and his family. He'd have to pay them so it was an expensive business, but he knew it was the only way to ensure I got the kind of work-out which would enhance my career.

Now, in 1988, it was the same story. One of my sparring partners for this fight was a young up and coming fighter who boxed at middleweight or super-middle. He was at least a stone heavier than me and he was tough. We paid him £100 a day for his services and he was worth every penny. He was booked for five days and in the very first round on the first day with his first punch he broke my nose!

I now had a big choice to make. It was a week before the Rova fight. If I told anyone, the fight would be postponed. If I didn't and went ahead I could be seriously injured. I decided to stay shtum. It meant sparring for five rounds a day for the rest of that week and hoping I would just get over the nose break without requiring any treatment. Thankfully, I got away with it but I wouldn't recommend it!

The man who landed that powerful punch, and many more that week, was none other than Chris Eubank!

****

Next up was a mandatory defence. By now I had built up quite a fearsome ring record. I'd fought 23 times, losing just once. And for a boxer who had once been described as lacking a killer punch, I'd amassed an enviable KO count. Half of my 22 victories had come inside the distance.

Within two days of despatching Rova, Mike Barrett announced that I would defend my International and Commonwealth titles against the highly-rated Londoner, Rocky Kelly. It was, explained Barrett, an important step on the way to an inevitable shot at the world title. "I'm proud of this one," he said, "as I think it is a contest that will fire the imagination of the fight public. Gary faces a tough assignment against Kelly. Both lads know only one way to fight and that is to go forward slinging punches. It will be total war."

Almost immediately rival promoter Frank Warren, who'd previously tried to derail my Commonwealth title challenge against Wilf Gentzen, suddenly burst on the scene with a counter offer. He announced that he was prepared to pay me £25,000 (more than treble my biggest pay day to date) to defend my title against his boy, George Collins. The crafty Barrett dismissed the idea out of hand yet left the door open by saying Collins might get a shot but only after the Kelly fight and only if the money on offer was good enough.

On 10th December 1988 I celebrated my 23rd birthday. Among the many goodwill messages was one from Rangers star Ian Ferguson. In our younger days we had both played for the Glasgow-based Aberdeen Boys club. Fergie had been following my career with great interest and phoned me at home to wish me Happy Birthday and invite me to Ibrox where he presented me with a card. Naturally, the papers were there to capture the moment. As they were a few days later when I bought a brand-new sports car as a gift to myself for having such a great year.

By now I wasn't just making the news. I was writing it, too. I had a weekly column in the *Jewish Herald* in which I had this to say about my forthcoming title defence, "Kelly's a tough customer. He's the number one contender not only for my Commonwealth title but also for Kirkland Laing's British crown. He's lost only twice in the last five years in 17 fights. Funnily enough he lost to Dave Douglas in 1983. Douglas is the only boxer to have beaten me. That was a bum verdict but I thrashed him in the return. I'll beat Kelly all right, because I'm better than him. If I don't I might as well pack it in. All I want is that world title."

In my next *Jewish Herald* column I revealed to my growing number of fans, "The fight date has been brought forward by seven days. So now it's on St Valentine's Day. But there won't be any love lost between me and Rocky. I'm going to give him a good thumping. Sure I'm confident. I've been training hard. I'm already running five or six miles every morning. Now I'm down here at Bath University for a couple of weeks before the fight where I train scientifically with former SAS man Tom Hudson. It's all hi-tec. From seven in the morning to six at night I run, swim, spar and do weights. They turn you into an athlete here. This is all on top of my conditioning over the last few years. I'm a dedicated fighter."

Kelly had been discovered by one of the most colourful men in British boxing, Harry Holland. Harry has the distinction of negotiating a fight promotion with the man who would one day become the President of the USA, but long before reaching those heady heights he was advertising for talent at the lower end of the pay scale.

In a 1985 ad Harry promised: "Any boxer on my promotions will receive minimum wages of: 6x2 min £200; 8x2 min £280; 6x3 min £300; 8x3 min £500; 10x3 min £900". It sounds like good money for the amount of time you'd spend in the ring but when you take into account the weeks of training it really doesn't add up to very much. Mind you, Harry claimed he lost more money than he ever made from boxing so that might explain the low rates.

He had certainly moved up in the world in the late 1990s when he joined a promotions company who tried to break into the big time. They wanted to put on a world title fight in Atlantic City and decided to invite a certain Donald Trump on board. Harry got the chance to put his case in person to the billionaire businessman, who politely declined the offer of investing in the fight game. Harry said later, "He told us we had no chance but that he admired our balls."

Meanwhile, much of the chat in the mainstream press about my future didn't concentrate on my forthcoming showdown with Kelly. Rather, it concerned Lloyd Honeyghan and, to a lesser extent, Simon Brown. Honeyghan, the WBC World Welterweight Champion, was firmly in my sights. Well, according to Mike Barret and Bobby Neill at any rate. Here's how the super-slick promoter/manager saw it: "Honeyghan's crown is the one we want. Gary will be the IBF Champion before the year is out and a fight against Honeyghan, with two world titles at stake, will break all box office records in this country."

Bobby Neill, who had trained Honeyghan to the world crown before an acrimonious split, added, "I felt so badly let down by Honeyghan that for a time I began to question my faith in the fight game. Honeyghan is an arrogant man and to be treated like that, after helping him to the title, hurt me deeply. But now I've got involved with Gary and he's totally restored my belief and brought all the old buzz back. Make no mistake, Gary has all the potential to become the world champion. We're hoping he will get his chance within a year. And if it's against Honeyghan that would be the ultimate dream."

I was also caught up in the 'bring on Honeyghan' mood. "I would love to have a crack at him. His walk-in style would suit me perfectly. I know I can beat him," I said.

There was, however, another boxer in the equation. One who had the potential, and desire, to destroy my dream. And that was Marlon Starling. On 4th February 1989 Lloyd Honeyghan defended his title against the American in Las Vegas. The outcome of this fight was of such importance to my camp that the three of us stayed up through the night, despite the time difference, listening to it on our radios and rooting anxiously for a British win.

There had been bad blood between the two for many months, as each had accused the other of avoiding him. The Englishman would have done well to have avoided Starling for a bit longer. By the ninth round Honeyghan had already been downed once, his jaw was badly swollen, his nose was bleeding and his right eye had started to swell. It came as no great surprise when the ref stopped the fight to save him from further punishment. That result ended one of my world title dreams. There was still Simon Brown... but only if I beat Rocky Kelly.

Any doubts about my ability to do just that evaporated at the first bell. Powerful and swift combinations of hooks and uppercuts with the left and right soon had Rocky on the rocks in what most commentators described as 'A Mini St Valentine's Day Massacre'. The challenger had entered the ring in Battersea looking confident. He had a holiday suntan and was resplendent in flamingo pink trunks. He brought with him a reputation for bravery and he more than lived up to that, much to the crowd's delight.

Round after round he pushed forward relentlessly but he had no defence against the forces of destruction that flew his way as I battered him time and again with brutal counter-punches. In the second round a cut appeared above Kelly's left eye. In the fourth he was knocked to the floor. By the sixth his face was covered in blood. So far he hadn't even come close to winning a round, yet still he doggedly marched forward, hoping for an unlikely breakthrough. But it was never going to happen. I was quite simply in a different league. I was in magnificent shape and form. The speed and power I unleashed left the crowd gasping in awe and Rocky rolling in agony.

The end of this one-sided affair came midway through the seventh. Following three unanswered body blows, a right upper-cut from me sent the courageous Kelly helplessly onto the ropes. Dazed, he tried to defend himself by holding on as my shots pounded into him from every angle. As two straight lefts slammed into his face a deep cut opened under his left eye. With a river of blood pumping out from the wounds the referee asked the doctor for an opinion. Nobody was surprised when he decided enough was enough.

Despite such a dazzling display of boxing brilliance I took the time and effort to pay tribute to my opponent. "That was a hard fight because Kelly was the official number one challenger and you don't get to that position unless you are good. He just kept on coming at me. If you're not fit he's the sort of fighter that'll have you. However, I never felt there was any point in the fight in which I didn't have control. I suppose you could say it was the hardest fight of the 24 I have had but in the end it went the way I predicted it would."

The beaten Rocky was full of praise for me. "If he continues his improvement he could go all the way to the world title and he does so with my best wishes."

And yet, despite making major strides forward - I was now combining great punching power with a more wary, experienced style - Bobby Neill was erring on the side of caution. "We're starting to get more leverage into his punches," he said, "he's learning to punch harder and he'll punch even harder because you need to be able to do this if you want to become world class."

Before the celebrations had died down, attention shifted to my next possible opponent. George Collins, unbeaten in 35 pro fights, was the name on everyone's lips.

George Collins

SOMETIME, WAY BACK in early 1986, the phone rang in Maurice Lewis's Glasgow home. On the line was Ernie Fossey, Frank Warren's right-hand man. He wanted to arrange a fight between me (entering my second year in the pros) and George Collins in London. Maurice listened carefully to the offer then replied, "Thanks Ernie but I'm really looking for something a bit more tasty than George Collins at this stage of Gary's career. Ideally I'm looking for someone a bit harder."

Maurice's comments were tongue-in-cheek. He knew fine well I was being lined up as cannon fodder for Collins, whose camp believed they'd win comfortably in their home town. Maurice, quite rightly, wanted no part of it. Collins, from Surrey, had been a phenomenal amateur, winning his first 67 fights. He was one victory away from entering the *Guinness Book of Records* when he got caught cold by Gary Stretch and was knocked out in the first round. It was his only defeat and by the time he turned pro in February 1985, just three months before me, his record was an incredible 77-1.

By March 1986 he'd won his first 12 professional fights, 9 within the distance, and his reputation was growing rapidly. Maurice told a pal that night that the two of us would meet one day, probably for a title. Now, three years down the line, his prophecy was about to come true. But before that could happen, I had a date in Budapest. Mike Barrett and I flew out to the Hungarian capital to watch IBF champ Simon Brown defend his crown against the tough Puerto Rican, Jorge Maysonet. Although it was six months before the fall of the Berlin Wall, and more than a year before Hungary's first free elections, the former Communist state was already in the process of emerging from behind the Iron Curtain. This was the first time fans there would see a world title fight involving non-Eastern Bloc boxers. As such it was a celebration of freedom and Mike and I were treated like minor royalty by the promoters, who presented us with a medal to commemorate the occasion.

Barrett was in Budapest to meet Brown's manager and discuss a title defence against me. He also wanted me to see a genuine world champion in action at close quarters. On both counts we came away virtually empty-handed. No deal was done and the classy Brown demolished his challenger with ease inside just three rounds. Although highly-impressed, I wasn't overawed by what I'd seen and returned to London still brimming with confidence.

The contract for my clash with Collins was signed by Barrett and Warren on Thursday 9th March 1989. The fight would take place 27 days later on Wednesday 5th April at the Royal Albert Hall. This would be Barrett's 150th show at the famous arena. It would also become one of the biggest domestic battles Britain had seen for years and was a guaranteed sell-out. There was no love lost between the pair of us. I felt Collins was extremely over-rated and I was furious at the way he was lauded as the golden boy of British boxing by London-based sportswriters. For his part Collins was raging because he had always believed I was an inferior fighter and had been avoiding him.

I didn't really know Collins, yet our paths had already crossed. On 27th January 1987, the night I won the Scottish title from Dave Douglas, George fought on the undercard. He was too good for Mexican Ariel Conde, gaining a second-round TKO. I didn't know or care who he was then and I couldn't hide my disdain for him now. Dave Douglas and George Collins shared the nickname "Gipsy" and I reckoned they would share the same fate against me.

Almost immediately after our fight was announced I

launched a bitter verbal volley at him. It was an uncharacteristic character assassination but I felt I had good reason. Normally I don't go in for all the hype associated with the fight game, the staring-out contests, the threats, etc. But with Collins it was different.

I told reporters, "There he stands, the big name, the guy with all the glitz and glamour. He's undefeated in 35 fights yet he wasn't even an area champion. All he's fought is a procession of duds. He's on TV all the time and still doesn't look good. He's always wobbling. Yet, would you believe, Collins makes out he doesn't even know my name. He couldn't even mention it properly the last time he was on television. But he'll know it the next time, I promise. When we meet it's going to be his loss, his problem. It'll be his 36th fight and finished. End of a glamorous career. My name will probably haunt him for the rest of his life."

My resentment was further exposed in my column for the *Jewish Herald*. "George Collins won't go five rounds when I take him on at the Royal Albert Hall. That's not just talk. I hate the guy. In fact, I must admit I'm a bit jealous. I've had to work hard to win my Commonwealth and WBC International Welterweight titles and I've hardly had any TV exposure. Collins has fought nobodies and has hardly been off the TV.

"Yes his record is good, 35 wins as a professional in 35 fights. But just look at the quality of his opponents. As an amateur he only lost one fight in 78 contests but that hardly matters now. I've won 23 out of 24 and the one I lost was disputed. I've fought in the States and won and fought in the Royal Albert Hall and won. And the way I took apart Rocky Kelly last month shows I'll have just too much skill, speed and strength against Collins.

"Sure, he'll be keyed up to take my titles but believe me he has no chance at all. This fight is going to put me on the map. You can't tell how good or bad Collins is. He's only ever fought eight-rounders. Collins has had it all his own way because he's had a good manager in Frank Warren. But I've got a good manager now in Mike Barrett. He knows the game inside out. He's done well for me over my last six fights.

"I'm more motivated for this punch-up than any other. I'm even training harder. In fact, so hard Bobby Neill is telling me to calm down. Collins has no chance. He's fought nobodies. He'll be yesterday's man by the time I'm finished with him."

As fight-night drew nearer I began to temper my public comments and adopt a more analytical approach. "I'm confident I'll win," I said, "but I think the fight will be a lot tougher than many people are saying. They say Collins has had it easy throughout his career so far. But nobody beats 35 opponents in a row without having something. And he knows this is his chance to prove the critics wrong. He'll be fired up for this one all right.

"Collins has only lost once in 111 fights as an amateur and professional so he has to be taken extremely seriously. This could easily be the hardest fight of my career. He's certainly a stylish stand-up fighter. As for his punching power, well you never know about that until you've been in with somebody."

Some observers were beginning to think I was backtracking. I wasn't. It was just part of a more mature approach that I had started to adopt. But the same couldn't be said for my management team. According to Mike Barrett, he was already looking beyond this fight to a money-spinning clash against Lloyd Honeyghan. He announced that he'd offered Honeyghan £50,000 to take me on.

In the programme for the show he wrote, "Gary has learned his trade. What he needs now is to broaden his experience against good fighters. Collins represents the first step. Honeyghan would be the logical follow on."

Bobby Neill was even more effusive. "In all the years I've been in this game," he said, "I've not come across anyone as dedicated or willing to learn as Gary. Gary has a lot of natural ability. I doubt there is anyone in Britain with his range of punches or his ability to read a fight. I could talk all night about his footwork, his balance, his reflexes. But the most important quality in Gary Jacobs is his willingness to learn. You can show him a move in the gym and he'll add it to his repertoire immediately. That's rare in any fighter and it's what puts Gary ahead of all of them. Over the years I've had some good fighters. Gary Jacobs is the most complete fighter I've ever trained."

Britain's boxing writers were obviously in complete agreement with Barrett and Neill, because just a week before the fight they voted me Best Young Boxer of the Year.

For his part, Collins wasn't letting the hype get to him. He wouldn't make any rash predictions. But he was confident enough to put £2,000 on himself at odds of 6/4 to win the fight and said, "I think I'm going to prove I'm a puncher. Jacobs is awkward and is very, very fit. But, after seeing him live and studying him on videos, I don't really rate him as a brilliant fighter. We're both going to be ready so I don't see it going the 12 rounds."

He couldn't have been more wrong. After 11 rounds of the pair of us standing toe-to-toe and slugging each other, at a Royal Albert Hall packed to the rafters, it looked as though I had done enough. Collins, who'd never previously fought at this level, certainly hadn't been outclassed. In the early rounds he consistently caught me with his pinpoint jabs and hooks. But by the fifth round I had cut the challenger above his left eye.

My dogged determination finally began to wear him down. In the 8th, two massive body shots had him gasping in pain. But, remarkably, he found the courage and strength to stay on his feet and keep plugging away. In the 11th, I landed a tremendous right-hander over the top which left him stunned, but still standing.

My superior strength and technique had led most neutral observers to conclude that I was a comfortable couple of rounds ahead going into the 12th. Barrett and Neill certainly thought so and advised me of their feelings in between rounds. "You've won the fight so stay out of trouble," they said.

But Maurice, who was also in the corner, wasn't so sure. He was worried. He'd seen the ref constantly ticking me off for low blows. Maurice thought the ref was being too critical so just before I re-entered the fray for the final time he whispered to me, "Try and put him down, son. You need this round to win it."

And with just over a minute to go I did just that. Ignoring the advice from Barrett and Neill, I relentlessly stalked my weakened prey and eventually cornered him before unleashing a barrage of fierce shots that forced Collins to his knees for a count of eight. There was no way back for the challenger but he gamely got up and kept battling to the final bell.

The referee awarded me the decision – by a margin of seven rounds to five. Maurice was spot on. Had Collins won the last round it would have been a draw.

It had been my toughest fight to date, yet there was not a mark on me. Collins, meanwhile, was battered, bloodied and bruised. But he'd earned my respect.

"The guy had a heart like a lion," I said afterwards. "He's an extremely good fighter and by getting up like that showed how game he was. He's the only good fighter I've ever met. I honestly don't know how he took some of those shots. Only his courage and fierce pride kept him on his feet. He certainly gave me one terrific fight."

It was one of the most exciting fights the Royal Albert Hall had seen for years. Surely now the London fight fans would regard me as a genuine contender.

Certainly, I had no doubts about my own ability.

I knew I was good when I won the Commonwealth title and with Bobby Neil by my side I was full of confidence.

I told one reporter, "He's the best trainer in the world. He knows how to turn a 'roughhouse' into a smooth fighting machine. We treat every fight the same: six weeks of running, weight training and sparring from seven in the morning. If the fight goes the distance, then I'm trained to go the distance.

"When I'm in the ring I hear the noise of the crowd and it gives me a lift but I'm oblivious to everything else. I have a job to do and I just get on with it. I know when I've landed a good punch because it feels clean.

"You know when you've fought a good fight but you never know you've won until the ref lifts your hand in the air."

At that stage I didn't believe there was anyone I couldn't beat. I knew that if they were put in front of me, I would find a way to beat them. That's why I chose boxing over a team sport, because it is all down to me in the ring whether I won or lost.

As for Collins, incredibly, although he lost to me, he was considered good enough to take on Kirkland Laing for the British title seven months later. He was still the golden boy in the eyes of many, although I knew better. He was brave, dedicated and talented, but not good enough at that level. I wasn't surprised when he lasted just five of the scheduled 12 rounds, losing on a TKO. It was his last fight.

Meanwhile, there was no word from Honeyghan's camp.

Into the Deep End

AFTER THE EXCITEMENT of the Collins fight I was hungry for another challenge and a bigger payday. Although the Royal Albert Hall was completely sold out and the action was shown live on TV right across the UK, I hadn't exactly earned a fortune for my hard-fought triumph in the Battle of Britain. I walked away with a mere £15,000 before expenses for the fight. I was now attracting plenty of money when I stepped into the ring, but very little of it was finding its way into my pocket.

Far from being greedy, boxing was my livelihood and like every other ambitious young sports person I wanted to maximise my earnings from what I knew would be a relatively short, and potentially hazardous, career. Perhaps sensing my frustration, Mike Barrett announced yet another ambitious project, which he suggested might involve me. He had negotiated a historic deal with the authorities in the Soviet Union which would give him the right to stage a professional show in Moscow for the first time.

This was May 1989, six months before the fall of the Berlin Wall. The Iron Curtain still existed, but only just. Barrett reckoned he would put on three world title fights in front of a 20,000 crowd in Moscow's Olympic Stadium, financed by American TV. He hoped I would be one of the contenders.

To prepare me, he arranged what he described as 'two stiff warm-ups'. The first would be back as top of the bill at the Royal Albert Hall on 27th June 1989, while the second would be sometime in August at a venue still to be decided.

My first opponent was Rollin Williams. On paper his credentials looked reasonable. He'd been a bit unfortunate only to earn a draw with Javier Suazo and he'd also held the USBA welterweight title, but closer inspection suggested Rollin was highly unlikely to give me a stern test. The draw with Suazo came about after an accidental head-butt which left Suazo with a deep cut on his left eye. The fight was stopped and because Williams was the culprit he could not win, even though he was ahead on all three scorecards. But that had been three years earlier. True, he went on to win the USBA title, but he'd since lost that.

Despite this questionable record, I didn't treat him lightly and trained just as hard for that fight as I had done for all the others. And right from the first bell I had him rocking and rolling all over the ring with a non-stop barrage of fierce shots from all angles. After just two minutes 47 seconds of the first round it was all over when the ref stepped in to end the American's torment. The only other incident of note that night occurred on the undercard as Lennox Lewis made a superb pro debut. The 1988 Super Heavyweight Olympic Gold Medallist knocked out Midlands area champion Al Malcolm after just 19 seconds of round two of a scheduled six. A right hand to the body and a left hook to the jaw sent Malcolm down in the opening minute. He got to his feet at the count of eight, and the fight continued. It was mainly one-way traffic, with the 31-year-old Malcolm being battered about the ring and he was a very relieved fighter when the bell sounded to end the round. In round two, Malcolm threw a hopeful right hand but took what looked like a gentle left jab to his right eye and stumbled forward to the canvas. He remained there, on his knees, with his eyes closed until ref Roy Francis counted him out.

Meanwhile, I was beginning to wonder about Mike Barrett's idea of a stiff warm-up! Also it crossed my mind that none of his grandiose plans for me had reached fruition. There was no big-money fight in Israel backed by an obscure billionaire, while the £50k deal with Lloyd Honeyghan had been quietly shelved and there was little, if any, progress in the American-

TV financed Soviet showdown in Moscow. I couldn't decide if he made these big announcements to keep up my spirits or to keep my name on the back pages!

However, those slight misgivings disappeared when he confirmed my next fight would be in New York City. There was no word of an opponent, though. What happened next would turn my world upside down and lead to a lasting friendship with a man who would go on to become one of the most controversial British fighters in recent years.

Meanwhile, I'd been busy making new friends in London. My flat in Swiss Cottage was situated above a wonderful Chinese restaurant called Singapore Gardens owned by the Lim family. It was run by their son Jeff, who soon became a good friend. I was a regular visitor and one day, after a fight the night before, I walked in for lunch sporting a large black eye. Old Mrs Lim quickly rushed over and told me she had the perfect cure for my problem. As I sat at the table she disappeared into the kitchen, returning soon after with a hard-boiled egg, which she proceeded to peel in front of me. She pressed the egg against my eye. Within a few moments the egg white had turned dark blue. She then told me to go the gents and look in the mirror. Amazingly, the darkness caused by the bruising had disappeared from my face. It was an old Chinese remedy and it worked every time!

I've been very lucky with friends. Most have stuck by me through thick and thin and are still with me to today. Gary Mann is a good example. We've been close pals since we used to chase girls together as teenagers. His late father Bernard was my first sponsor. Even before my very first amateur fight in Glasgow he took me to a sports shop in The Trongate and paid for a couple of tracksuits and tee shirts for me. He didn't want anything in return, he did it just to help me on my way.

When I was younger I would spend most weekends with Gary and often I'd sleep over at his house. I used to look forward to that, because his mother, Viv, made the best chicken soup in the world. Later, as my career took off, I kept going back for more. Whenever I was in Glasgow I would invite myself round there on a Friday night just for a bowl-full.

Gary also introduced me to a novel way of relaxing before my fights. He came to all my London boxing nights and most times the routine was the same. In the afternoon, after lunch, we'd head back to the Swiss Cottage flat and sit down for a friendly game of backgammon. We would play for small stakes for a few hours and it would take my mind off what was about to happen that evening. It was great fun and I usually won the money, although I've heard Gary tell folk he let me win on purpose. Anybody who knows him would dispute that!

Syd Rose and his son Peter are another great example. Peter decided against following in his father's footsteps into the jewellery trade and now runs his own very successful dog grooming and training business in Glasgow. Apart from sponsoring me, Syd went to every one of my fights and he always enjoyed a party afterwards. In Glasgow there would always be a big post-fight get-together at his house, where he was a great and generous host. Outwith Glasgow there was always a lavish do at a hotel or nightclub.

In London we'd go to the likes of Tramps, Blondes, Stringfellows and everybody would let their hair down. Many of my Glasgow mates like the Roses, Gary Mann, Alan Morris, Brian Ferguson, Alan Egelnick and Martin Newman would head south to support me and they'd all celebrate a victory with my London pals like Jeff Lim and Gary and Graham Sulkin. I told them that in the highly unlikely scenario of me losing a fight, they could still party the night away, except I wouldn't show up.

Indeed Graham Sulkin and I became such good pals that my next fight almost ended his marriage. I was due to take on Tyrone Moore of Louisville on Thursday 24th August at the Felt Forum in New York. Graham had arranged sponsorship for me by getting me free accommodation at the Concorde

Hotel in The Catskill Mountains. He and a few other pals came out to support me. Graham had written to the hotel, which had a massive Jewish clientele, and they agreed to give us a couple of weeks' accommodation free of charge.

By going there I joined an illustrious group of boxers who had used their facilities as a training camp in the lead-up to big fights. The list includes Emile Griffiths, Joe Frazier and Muhammad Ali. It should have cost us $1,000 a week each, but eight of us stayed there for a fortnight on the house! The only payment they insisted was a healthy gratuity for the staff.

Suddenly, just two days before the fight, Mike Barrett told me he wanted to change the plans. He proposed that I should fight Buddy McGirt instead. It would be a top-of-the-bill clash to be shown live from the Felt Forum in Madison Square Gardens on American TV. McGirt and I would both be last minute stand-ins. The original top-of-the-bill bout should have been WBA lightweight champion Edwin Rosario's title defence against Lupe Suarez. But the champ tore a ligament on the knuckle of his right index finger in training postponing the fight. TV, promoters and sponsors were all desperately scratching around for a replacement and were prepared to pay big bucks to ensure the show went ahead.

McGirt was a few classes above my original opponent. He'd been a pro for seven years and had only lost twice in that time. His record was amazing. He had made his pro debut in March 1982 when he drew a four-rounder with Lamont Haithcoach. He then went on an unbeaten four-and-a-half year run of 29 fights which included 25 knock-outs. He suffered his first defeat in July 1986 against Frankie Warren but recovered to win the next ten with eight KOs. He'd then avenged the Warren defeat winning the vacant IBF lightweight title in February 1988. McGirt then successfully defended that title against Howard Davis Junior, who had lost to Jim Watt at Ibrox Park in June 1980, when they fought for the vacant WBC lightweight crown. In his next defence he lost the title to Meldrick Taylor, before bouncing back with five wins on the trot.

So I was being asked to take on a vastly more experienced former world champion. It was a high-risk proposition. But I had no hesitation and agreed immediately. There was an extra consideration. I would earn $50,000 for stepping into the ring, my biggest payday by far. In addition, I was in superb condition and scared of no-one.

The new arrangements caused problems for Graham, though. He phoned his wife Jan and said, 'you'll never guess, it's unbelievable, Gary's fighting on Sunday'. Graham was due to fly back to London on Friday because there was an important family get-together the next day.

Jan responded, 'what a shame you'll miss it. We're going out on Saturday'.

But Graham was adamant about staying to watch my fight and told Jan he'd be back on Monday. Suddenly his hotel phone went dead. So he re-dialled Jan and asked her if they accidentally got cut off. She said, 'no and don't call me again,' before slamming the phone down!

As for the fight, I was quietly confident I'd do well. Mike Barrett reckoned it was a fantastic prime time TV opportunity and victory would hand me a major breakthrough in America. Back in Scotland, Ken Buchanan wrote a newspaper article suggesting that I could beat McGirt. It was a view not shared by many American experts and they, as it turned out, knew exactly what they were talking about.

On the night I was outclassed by a better fighter but I wasn't disgraced. McGirt didn't manage to knock me out, as he had done with 35 previous opponents, but there's no denying it, he beat me easy. Right from the first bell I found it very hard to land a proper punch, while he seemed able to hit me with ease. He was fast, hard and too clever for me. After ten rounds the judges and ref gave him a comfortable points victory.

I put on a brave face in public, but privately I now knew

I had a very long way to go if I wanted to reach world class status. And for the first time in my life doubts about my ability began to creep in. McGirt was clearly already operating at a higher level and perhaps it was a bit hasty to go in against him so early in my career, even though the money on offer had been incredible.

But what really worried me was that after the fight I didn't rate McGirt that highly. He was a counter-puncher who picked me off at will and was way too good for me at that stage of my career. He just had too many tools in the bag, yet I didn't see him as a world class fighter, he didn't dominate throughout and there were times when I was on top. Yet if he could beat me so easily, what did it say about my prospects?

While these mixed emotions provided me with a great deal to think about on the long flight home, unbeknown to me there were a number of positives to emerge from the defeat. For a start, I would soon realise that losing this fight would, in a strange way, become a launch pad for a highly-successful career.

My relationship with Mike Barrett had begun to deteriorate slightly before this trip. We were now drifting further apart. The night before the fight he and Bobby Neil wanted me to watch a video of Buddy McGirt in action. But I refused. My reason was simple. I only knew one way to box and that was going forward with aggression looking to land heavy punishing blows on my opponent. I couldn't change my style even if I wanted to. So I had nothing to gain by watching the video and said it was a waste of time. Mike Barrett later described my actions as, "yet another example of Gary's arrogance."

Graham Sulkin, whose judgement I respected absolutely by now, was unhappy at the turn of events and challenged Mike Barrett's thinking about McGirt. My manager's response added fuel to the fire when he said he thought I could take McGirt. Graham concluded that Barrett had seriously underestimated my opponent. It was a view that was difficult to argue against. That heated discussion was the start of the process which would eventually lead me to a new management team and an exciting new chapter in my career.

Chris Eubank And Schoolboy Scraps

MY PERFORMANCE against McGirt had made a big impression on a fellow fighter who was destined for the big time. Chris Eubank, who'd become a pal since we'd sparred together before my fight with Rova nine months earlier, was highly impressed. Although many years would pass before I found out why.

It was in the summer of 2010 when we met up in London to reminisce that he finally told me, "I walk with a code of ethics as a warrior. You, Gary, are a warrior like me. That's why you are my friend. The people on the inside, like me, know your calibre. Calibre is heart. Fighting Buddy McGirt would be the equivalent of me fighting Roy Jones. I would never go looking for Roy Jones. Why? Because that wouldn't be intelligent. If you beat him it's only a notch. But you're going to lose years off your life by fighting him. Win or lose, the man's going to damage you. Buddy McGirt would have damaged you. You may not see it but I would know that. You can't get in there with a man like Buddy McGirt and not get damaged.

"McGirt was the highest calibre fighter. You have to understand that he was the welterweight division's equivalent of Mike Tyson, or Marvin Hagler or Sugar Ray Leonard. He was that brilliant. And when you fought a man like that you proved you were one of the few with heart."

I was stunned, but not half as stunned as he was when I told him for the first time how he had broken my nose!

Chris is one of the most colourful characters British boxing has ever produced and has been at the heart of several highly-controversial moments. Perhaps none more so than on 18th March 1995 when he lost his WBO Super-Middleweight title to Steve Collins and afterwards accused the Irish challenger of "legal cheating". Although it is nearly 30 years since the affair, fight fans are still fiercely divided about the ins and outs of what took place.

At a pre-bout press conference Collins stated that he'd been hypnotised and would feel no pain from any of Eubank's punches. This was apparently backed up by Dr Tony Quinn, the so-called hypnotist. Earlier, at the weigh-in, Collins claimed that due to being hypnotized he couldn't be hurt and that he wouldn't bleed in the ring.

In a TV interview it was then put to Dr Quinn that if Collins had been mentally conditioned to feel no pain then it would be a big worry because the Irishman could continue to battle on through the pain threshold and suffer some damage as a consequence, saying, "It's true he will feel less pain than he normally would, that's definitely true. He'll also find that he is able to move much easier. When he sees punches coming in they'll look three times slower than normal. We've also made the target three times bigger. So it's much easier for him to be aware of what's happening."

He told other reporters, "My name is Tony Quinn and I am a doctor of clinical hypnosis and I've been working with Steve for the past month . . . when Eubank hits him, I've ensured Steve will not feel any pain."

This had a serious impact on Chris, who wanted to pull out of the fight. He said: "This is not right. How can I fight a man who has been hypnotised? He will not feel pain. This is dangerous. It is wrong."

Chris had every right to be deeply concerned. Four years earlier he had knocked out Michael Watson in the final round of a brutal rematch. Watson, who was leading on the scorecards of all three judges when he was KO'd, was in a coma for 40 days. He needed six brain operations to remove a blood clot and spent a year in intensive care. For the first eight months he couldn't hear, speak, or walk. He left hospital in a wheelchair which he needed for another six years before he eventually recovered all of those functions.

Nobody knows how the tragic events of that night impacted on Chris's psyche. But here's a statistic to consider: In his 28 fights leading up to the ill-fated encounter with Michael Watson Chris scored 16 knock-outs. In his next 15 fights he produced only four. It might be argued that his desire to completely annihilate his opponent had disappeared. As one commentator put it: "the appetite for winning remained but the appetite for destruction had gone."

All this was swirling round Chris's head when, just three weeks before his clash with Collins, another tragedy in the ring must have shaken him still further. American Gerald McClellan suffered a massive blood clot to the brain and needed emergency surgery lasting three-and-a-half-hours to remove it. The American had been injured while challenging Nigel Benn for his WBC Super Middleweight title at the London Arena. He was still in a coma by the time the Eubank v Collins clash came around. He would remain in that state for a total of two months but emerged brain-damaged, blind, with his hearing impaired and unable to walk. To further confuse the issue Benn, who had been knocked down twice by McClellan, was heard thanking his hypnotist in a post-fight interview.

It's impossible to guess how much all this affected Chris, but he lost against Collins despite the fact most observers thought he should have won on the night. It was a difficult subject and although I was keen to hear his thoughts, I diplomatically decided not to broach it. Instead, we talked about our childhood and we both realized that our earliest experiences were very similar. Like me, Chris was fighting from a very early age and once he started, it became increasingly difficult to stop.

I had my first taste of battling by the time I was three. Ironically, at the time, my family lived in an area of Glasgow ironically called "Battlefield". My parents, Alan and Avril, still remember the day I came home with tears streaming down my face. In between loud gasping sobs I managed to blurt out that the boy in the upstairs tenement flat had attacked me.

My mother and father were less than sympathetic. "Stop crying and hit him back," was their somewhat harsh response. I took that message to heart and have been hitting back, with considerable force and painful consequences, ever since. The wee boy upstairs was the first to experience my newly-discovered philosophy of life.

The next day his mother battered on our front door screaming that I had badly beaten up her son. My parents didn't know that her son had attacked me with a stick (I rarely told them the whole story). Following their advice I had found my own stick and went looking for vengeance. Except my stick had a big nail in it!

Around the time I was born my father, Alan, had started his own furniture removal business. It prospered and soon we were on the move to a bigger house in a smarter neighbourhood. But relocating upmarket into a cushier environment had no impact on my warrior-like ways.

At Netherlee Primary I began got a bad name as a brawler. This reputation would follow me throughout school, although in my opinion there was usually a very good explanation for my occasional brutish behaviour.

There were two major incidents which illustrate the point. The first happened when we were living in Stamperland. As usual, my parents were the last to hear about it when something went wrong. One night a guy came to the door with his son and angrily told my dad that I had given his boy a hiding. He wanted to know what my father proposed doing about it.

My father, who knew nothing about this, called me over and when I came to the door the other parent took one look at me and said, "No not him, it was your bigger boy. Call your bigger boy to the door."

My father responded, "I don't have a bigger boy. I've got a smaller boy but this is the biggest boy I've got." The guy looked at me then looked at his own son who was twice my size and smacked him across the face before apologising and leaving with a disgusted look on his face.

It turned out the bigger boy had stolen my bike and I retrieved it in my own special way. My parents couldn't complain and they didn't. After all I was just fighting back the way they had always encouraged me.

The next time I got into trouble at Netherlee there was a more sinister scenario. My parents were summoned to see the headmaster. I had badly beaten a boy in the playground. He didn't need hospital treatment but he had a couple of pretty serious black eyes and plenty of sore bits dotted about his body. I was asked to explain myself at a meeting in the head's office. It turns out this boy had called my brother, Steven, who is three years younger than me, a 'Jewish bastard.' I was standing nearby in the playground and either the boy didn't notice me or didn't know we were brothers. It didn't matter. I went for him and hurt him. The boy's parents complained and initially it looked as if I was going to get suspended. But when the headmaster heard my side of the story he agreed with me and even told me I hadn't hit the racist boy hard enough.

That was my first experience of antisemitism. It, and many other similar incidents which followed, had a profound impact on me. Most Jews will tell you they don't encounter much antisemitism in the West of Scotland, where the vast majority of religious tension is created and maintained by the bigotry and loathing which divides some Roman Catholics and Protestants. But I suffered more than most from anti-Jewish attacks. The perpetrators soon learned to their cost, though, that some Jews fight back. But it was far from an enjoyable experience for anyone involved.

I was always fighting at school but it was a terrible existence. At that stage of my life I genuinely hated all the conflict. There was, however, no other way. As my dad's business improved we kept moving to bigger and better houses and I was going to different schools: all of a sudden you're the new guy. As a new boy going to a new school, I was always having to prove myself, always fighting all the hard men in the school who want to take you on. It really was horrible.

I had to fight at school because if I didn't people would walk all over me. And it was all down to the Jewish thing, because of the name Jacobs. One hundred percent the reason. They used to goad me by calling me "Jewboy". Or saying, "where Jew come from" and, "I know Jew." To make matters worse I was a wee guy. So I must have looked like a pushover to the bigger bullies. Boy, were they in for a massive and agonising shock.

I never looked for fights, never started them but I would always fire in at full force once they got going. Maybe, if I hadn't had such a Jewish name, it would have been easier and my life would have been different. I stood up for myself and didn't hold back once it started. I didn't go looking for trouble, yet trouble had no difficulty tracking me down. Especially on the day of the showdown at Tinkers, which is a small play park not far from Clarkston Toll on the Old Mearns Road.

Nobody knows why it's called Tinkers but one fine day I fought four other boys there in quick succession, emerging victorious and unscathed like a battle-hardened Roman Gladiator.

By now I had graduated to the highly-respected Williamwood High School. One afternoon my parents knew something unusual had happened but, as usual, couldn't prise the details from me. I was stubborn that way. When I got home from school it was much later than normal. My tie was halfway round my neck, my trousers were torn and dirty and my shirt was ripped. But I'm proud to say there was not a mark on my body.

My mother hasn't forgotten that day. She would tell a friend, "He was always fighting and it cost us a fortune to keep replacing his school uniform. He never admitted it, always saying he was playing. This time we knew he'd been in a big fight but it was years later before we learned the truth."

Alan Buchanan was one of the main protagonists and, many years on, the events are still fresh in his mind. Looking back on that day he remarked recently, "I don't know how Gary did it. How he found the strength and courage to carry on against such odds. I don't know anybody else who could have done it. Everybody recognised him in first year at Williamwood. He had a reputation as a bit of scrapper, a fighter always getting into bother. Everyone perceived him as really arrogant and ignorant. I remember this cocky wee guy who swaggered about the place. I was also a bit full of myself so it didn't bother me but it annoyed a lot of people. He came with a bad reputation because he got into trouble all the time at Netherlee.

"One day Gary insulted my girlfriend and I decided to defend her honour. We were in first year. It was something ridiculous, something stupid. But when you're a wee kid these things seem important at the time. So it was a case of 'see you after school'. There was a buzz going round the corridors and classrooms all afternoon - Buckie's fighting Jake. We ended up fighting three times in the space of 40 minutes. The first two were broken up by teachers and passers-by. The third, at Tinkers, ended when we agreed to call it quits. Neither of us could defeat the other and we realised there was no point carrying on.

"I began walking away when I heard a commotion. I turned and saw Gary fighting again. He and I had been wrestling for the best part of an hour and I know I was completely knackered. He would have been as well. A few of the so-called hard men in the school must have decided to take advantage of the situation and thought this was the best time to attack Gary. One had a go, egged on by the others. But it didn't take long for Gary to subdue him. He hardly had any time to draw breath when another boy attacked him. Gary sorted him too. I couldn't believe he still had the strength to deal with these two.

"There must have been a line of people waiting to take him on because, incredibly, a third boy then jumped on Gary. But once again the wee man emerged victorious. After that Gary just stood there, not even breathless, scowling at everyone, daring them to have a go. He would have fought all day, but by now, after what they'd witnessed, nobody would go near him. He turned into a legend that day.

"Before that day I'd heard only that he was an ignorant, arrogant wee boy who liked to fight and noise people up. From then on he and I became great mates and still are to this day. I think after that he was accepted more by the rest of the school. I'm sure the antisemitism stoked some of the fires in him. He's quite sallow-skinned with jet black hair, the archetypal wee kind of Jewish bloke, especially with the prominent nose. But it was never an issue with me. I was just defending my girl's honour.

"Gary still had to scrap now and again but from then on very few willingly took him on. People had seen the strength in him. I was exhausted and I know he was too but he had to carry on. He wouldn't let himself get his face kicked in."

I was always fighting at Tinkers. It became a home away from home for me. At Williamwood it was just terrible, I was fighting all the time. Today, if you ask all these other people I was at school with, they'd probably say he was fighting so much as a kid I knew he'd become a professional fighter or a boxer eventually because that was what he did at school and that it was inevitable. Yet a career as a fighter wasn't something that I thought about at the time. Getting hit and hitting back was just a way of life in those days. It was forced on me.

Sometimes the violence on my part went too far and someone else went home in pain. Other times I got hurt. But I didn't sit down to analyse it. I didn't appear to have any control of events in school. The fights just happened.

Eventually I settled down at secondary school, helped by a growing number of pals like Alan Buchanan. But, just as I began to find life a bit easier, the family was on the move again. The furniture removal business was booming and after just six months at Williamwood, my parents bought a fancy new house in the affluent suburb of Newton Mearns. This meant yet another school, Mearns Castle, and yet another battle to overcome my bad boy reputation.

Antisemitism was rife at the new school and that meant more action for me. There were quite a lot of Jewish kids at Mearns Castle and they pretty much kept themselves to themselves. They weren't generally bullied, more victimised. From time to time some of them were taunted and verbally abused but none of them ever spoke back or stood up for themselves. They just took it. I was furious with that and decided to do something about it. From that point on I decreed that an attack on any Jew in the school would be interpreted as an attack on me. Even if it wasn't aimed at me I was going to take it personally. To me the attackers were just bullies who needed to be taught a lesson. And I was just the boy to do the teaching!

You see, by now, after so many fights, I had developed a bit of a taste for it. That approach soon led to plenty of trouble and it wasn't long before I was reprimanded. I beat up a boy who insulted a girl for being Jewish. I was suspended but the other boy was expelled. My exposure to antisemitism wasn't restricted to the school playground. As a teenager I joined a Jewish youth club in Giffnock called Maccabi whose football team played in the local amateur league. It wasn't long before I got a game – and into more hot water.

My friend Martin Newman and I were in the team at the same time and every Sunday afternoon we'd be insulted by our opponents and their supporters on the sidelines. It happened simply because we were Jewish, regardless of the score. It wouldn't happen nowadays - you can imagine the public outrage - but back then nobody was willing to stop it. I used to complain to the referees but nothing happened. By the end of the games I was always in a blind fury.

Martin, a close pal from our days together at Netherlee Primary, concurs, "I don't think we ever played a game where we weren't subjected to antisemitic remarks from either players in the opposing team or their fans or sometimes a combination of both."

In the worst example, an opposing player turned to me and said, "It's a fuckin pity Hitler missed you." When I protested to the ref I was met with a shrug of the shoulders and the response, "Ach, he's only joking." I didn't see the funny side and next time the ref turned his back the racist got a punch on the nose.

My act of religious retribution provoked fury from the opposition and their watching fans, who were usually proud parents who should have known better but either didn't or chose not to. But the man in black claimed he hadn't seen anything, brushed aside their protests and waved play on.

Around six months later, when I was in second year at Mearns Castle, my parents decided to move house again, this time to Australia. My dad sold the removal company for good money and the five of us (I have a younger brother and sister who are twins) headed Down Under for a new life in the sun. In Australia my dad was working for an airline company moving cargo around the country. We were living the good life in Sydney. We'd rented a very nice big house which even in those days was worth a million dollars. The new opulent surroundings and the long hot sunny days seemed to work wonders for me. For the first time in my life nobody picked on me for being Jewish. It may have been a coincidence but suddenly I wasn't fighting any more.

Not everybody benefited from the move, though. The Maccabi team Martin and I joined had been the league's perpetual whipping boys. But we were very strong characters and soon added steel to the team's weak backbone. Martin in the heart of the defence and me in midfield. It wasn't long before our influence turned the Jewish team from losers to winners. However that came to an abrupt end with my move overseas.

When I emigrated to Australia, Maccabi had been top of the league. There were two games to go and we needed a win and a draw to be champions for the first time. When I was in Australia I heard they'd lost them both, conceding 28 goals in the process!

Yet it wasn't all sweetness and light in Sydney. The constant upheaval had seriously disrupted my education. Matters came to a head in Australia, where the schools were way behind their Scottish counterparts. In the classroom I was getting bored to the point of insanity. And, of course, there was a fight. Not just any old fight but one which would leave its mark on me for the rest of my life.

I don't remember much about the incident but I ended up in hospital after getting hit in the face by a boy with an iron bar. A few days earlier my dad noticed my knuckles were badly bruised and asked me what happened to my hand. I told him I'd got into a fight with a guy and had him pinned down on the deck pummelling his face. The guy moved his head, I missed his face and punched the living daylights out of the pavement.

A few days later the guy crept up on me and smashed me with an iron bar right across the nose. I didn't see it coming. Today no-one remembers how it all started but there was no long-running feud and, despite the seriousness of the assault, the police weren't involved. It was my only fight in Australia, yet the ferocity of the attack left my nose broken beyond repair despite the surgeon's best efforts. However, my mis-shapen nose would play a major role in shaping the rest of my life.

That injury apart, I settled down in Australia and began enjoying life. I left school and got a job, working in a motel cleaning bedrooms, making beds and sweeping floors. It might not have sounded very glamorous but for a 15-year-old with no qualifications the pay, $200 a week, was brilliant.

I continued my love affair with football and eventually signed a contract with one of the top local sides, Sydney City. I spent a year in their reserves and enjoyed every minute of it. However, my happiness was short-lived. A year into our sojourn in the sunshine my dad returned to Glasgow for a holiday and realised he was terribly homesick.

Within another 12 months we were all back in Glasgow, where we settled into a smart flat in Tantallon Road, Shawlands, just across from Queen's Park. It was October 1982. We'd been in Australia for two years and I was two months away from turning 17. I found work as an apprentice kitchen fitter with a local firm who also employed my uncle. I was earning £40 a week and had never even considered boxing as a sport, never mind a way of life.

One fateful day we were visited by Rosemary Lewis who was a neighbour. She had recently become friendly with my parents, meeting them shortly after they had arrived from Australia. It was the first time she'd set eyes on me and I made a big impression on her. She told me some time later that I reminded her of a panther.

She said later, "You were lying out on the couch like a panther. I can't explain why I thought you looked like one. You were fully clothed and just reminded me of one. I reckoned you were about 19 or 20 years old because you looked so strong. But what really captured my attention was your nose. There was a scar on it which made me think you had broken it while boxing."

Rosemary asked me that night if I had been boxing and, to her surprise I said no. Then my father explained about the fight in Australia. Before leaving Rosemary told me that her husband Maurice was involved in the fight game and suggested I visit him, that I might enjoy boxing. To this day Rosemary doesn't know why she made that suggestion. But I remember thinking about it then deciding against it.

A few minutes later my father walked in and said, "£50 a fight! That's how much you'll get if you become a boxer," and suddenly I began taking the idea a lot more seriously. I was working a whole week just to earn £40 and I could get more than that for doing something that was one of my favourite pastimes. After all, I had always enjoyed a good fight!

That night I knocked on Rosemary's door and from that moment on our lives would never be the same again…

Under New Management

After the McGirt fight, Mike Barrett decided that it would be better for me to get the defeat out of my system as soon as possible. He knew I hadn't been physically hurt by McGirt and that I was still in great shape. While I agreed with his strategy it did occur to me that Mike was choosing my opponents in a completely different way than Maurice Lewis did. After my only previous loss, to Dave 'Gipsy' Douglas, Maurice lined me up for a couple of guaranteed easy victories in a bid to boost my morale. In complete contrast Mike arranged for me to defend my Commonwealth crown against tough Canadian challenger Donovan Boucher, who'd lost only three times in 23 fights. The one saving grace was the fight, on 23rd November 1989, would take place in Scotland.

It should have been a straightforward defence, but 48 hours before I entered the ring at Motherwell Civic Centre a major row broke out when Boucher's manager, Raymond Rutter, accused Mike Barrett of bending the rules. The problem started when Barrett, who was also the promoter, announced that Londoner Roy Francis would referee the fight, and that he would be the sole official.

Rutter protested immediately saying, "It's outrageous that you are able to declare who will referee this contest 48 hours before it takes place. It is wrong that only the referee is in charge. In other countries where Commonwealth title fights have taken place three judges have taken control."

I wasn't particularly concerned about these wrangles. As usual I intended to do my talking in the ring. Victory would go a long way towards re-establishing my claim for a world title crack. Mike was already briefing reporters that my next fight would probably be a defence of my WBC International title against Venezuelan Luiz Garcia in Glasgow. He had already pencilled it in for February 1990, just three months away, and was talking about it as a potential final eliminator for the WBA world title held by American Mark Breland.

But first I would have to take care of Boucher. Ominously for me my opponent appeared equally focussed. The Jamaican-born Canadian sounded confident, almost cocky, when he told reporters in Glasgow, "I'm not worried in the least about this and will be delighted to welcome you all to Canada for my first defence after I have beaten your champion."

Sadly for me Donovan was spot on. After 12 rounds I had lost a close encounter on points to someone I believed to be a vastly inferior opponent. I just couldn't get my act together, was strangely lethargic and didn't land nearly enough punches. The ref, whose appointment was regarded as controversial, gave the decision to Boucher and scored it 118.5-117 in his favour.

After the fight I was bewildered, battered and bruised. But what really hurt was my ego. Boucher was good. After he took my Commonwealth title he went on to defend it successfully five times, defeating Kirkland Laing and Mickey Hughes in the process before losing his sixth defence to Eamonn Loughran, who would go on to become world welterweight champion. So, clearly, he had enough skill and firepower to mix it with some useful fighters. Despite that, deep down I knew I was better than him. Yet that night I was just not firing on all cylinders and I didn't know why. Something was seriously wrong and unless I could get to the bottom of it my world title dreams would be over.

Mike Barrett still believed in me, even though he described my performance as "appalling". He said, "Gary has got to develop more power. In his last two fights he has stood on leaden feet and been hit too often. Tonight he has tried to knock his man out and hasn't had the punch to do it."

In the dressing room the reality of the situation set in. Not only had I lost my Commonwealth title, my WBC International crown was also about to be taken from me, even though it wasn't at stake. My defeat meant it would become vacant. I was so depressed I told reporters that I didn't deserve to hold either title. But I've never been one to stay down in the dumps for long and thanks to encouragement from my family and friends I was soon back in the gym, training as hard as ever.

My next bout was chosen more carefully. There was no way I was going to lose three in a row.

But in what was becoming a regular feature of my career, my original opponent couldn't make it and another stepped in at short notice. Initially I was scheduled to meet former French champion Alain Cuvillier, but a couple of days earlier he was mugged in the street in his hometown near Paris. Alain was attacked by three men. One had a hammer and smashed up his knee, leaving him on crutches. He was replaced by fellow countryman Pascal Lorcy, who, coincidentally, had been beaten by Cuvillier when they fought for the French welterweight title two years earlier.

Once again Mike Barrett was talking up my chances, although anyone reading between the lines would find clear signs of a growing rift between us. My manager told the media, "Gary was very down after losing his title but he took a rest, thought about his future and the zest is back. Gary felt he could beat anyone in the world. He got big-headed but has now come back down to earth."

Mike may have been right about me, but there was no need to share these thoughts in public. The change of opponent didn't worry me unduly, even though as a southpaw he would be more awkward to deal with. I had been sparring with left-handers and had no fear of them. On the night Lorcy didn't last long. After two short rounds it was all over when the referee stopped the fight. Lorcy had been cut by some ferocious punching as I strove to get my recent defeats out of my system. I still believed I had what it took to become a world class fighter. But a measure of the task facing me was the choice of venue for this victory. In just eight months I'd gone from performing at Madison Square Gardens to Latchmere Leisure Centre in Wandsworth!

There was talk afterwards of me taking on Kirkland Laing for his British and European titles, but that would have to wait, because first I needed to get past tough Londoner Mickey Hughes. The fight was scheduled for 9th May, just 13 days after the Lorcy fight because the Frenchman had taken very little out of me and I was still super-fit. However, it would become yet another highly-controversial match-up.

Hughes, who'd been a great amateur and fought at the LA Olympics, had struggled to make his mark as a pro. But I knew I had to take him seriously. Unfortunately, he couldn't make the weight and was forced to pull out. His camp had asked for the rules to be relaxed but we, quite rightly, refused. There was a bit of an argument and heated words were exchanged. Suddenly, through no fault of mine, there was a fair amount of bad feeling between us, but I'd have to put those thoughts to one side and concentrate on taking on yet another last-minute substitute.

Mike Durvan graciously and courageously stepped in at just three hours' notice as an opponent. He knew what to expect and so did everybody else. He lasted just one minute 46 seconds before being knocked out. The poor performance on his part wasn't his fault. In boxing terms he should never have been within 500 miles of me, never mind in the same ring. Afterwards he admitted, "I've never been hurt so bad, it took my breath away."

The fight wasn't a complete waste of time. There was the bonus that I was back at the Royal Albert Hall. It was the UK's top venue and it's where I felt I belonged. Ironically, I was now on the undercard while Lennox Lewis topped the bill, with the transformation in our relative fortunes taking less than 11 months to unfold. This was Lennox's tenth triumph on the trot and he continued his winning ways for another 15 fights, picking up the WBC World Heavyweight title along the way. He successfully defended it three times before facing American Oliver McCall. The pair would become embroiled in two of the most extraordinary fights in modern heavyweight history.

The first time they met, McCall ended Lewis's unbeaten run with a sensational knock out. Prior to the fight at Wembley Arena in September 1994 Lewis had dismissed his opponent as "a sparring partner." The world champion had comfortably won the first round when, just 31 seconds into the second, McCall landed a thunderbolt right hand to the champ's nose. Lewis went down and although he was up after a count of six, his legs were wobbly and the referee ended the fight.

Lewis, the hot favourite, was raging afterwards claiming he was robbed by a lucky punch. The ref, José Guadalupe Garcia, replied, "To allow more punches to Lewis could have had fatal consequences. My duty is to protect the health of the boxer." McCall, who earned $1m as opposed to Lewis's $3.5m, said afterwards that he had been trying to catch his opponent with that right hook from the opening bell, adding that Mike Tyson had advised him to do so.

So the stage was set for a rematch, but both boxers had to wait until February 1997 for that to happen. By now, due to contractual wrangles, the WBC heavyweight title was vacant. This time McCall would get the lion's share of the purse, even though Lewis was still the hot favourite. Doubts about McCall's mental state and the quality of his preparations had emerged about eight months before the fight, when he was arrested in July 1996 on charges of possessing crack cocaine and marijuana. The following month he entered rehab. In December he was arrested again after he threw a Christmas tree in a hotel lobby and spat on a police car and returned to rehab. A few days later Don King, McCall's promoter, confirmed he would be fit to fight Lewis, even though he was in treatment.

The fight began as expected with Lewis taking charge in the first three rounds. But at the end of the third, McCall stunned the 4,500 plus crowd at the Las Vegas Hilton by refusing to return to his corner, preferring, instead, to walk around the ring. In the fourth, McCall threw just two punches and when the round ended, referee Mills Lane took him by the arm and led him to his corner. At that stage McCall burst into tears. Less than a minute into the fifth, with McCall throwing just one punch, the ref stopped the fight. The blame game started almost immediately after the fight.

Referee Mills Lane said, "I think the young man really needs to talk to someone in the mental health field," while WBC president Jose Sulaiman stated that he believed McCall had suffered a nervous breakdown. McCall's trainer, George Benton, added, "Lewis was in there with a lunatic. McCall was talking incoherently, but he had been doing that all week. It started a long time ago, and I think it caught up with him."

Meanwhile promoter Dino Duva added, "Don King should have never made him available to fight. He was in no condition to mentally or physically fight. We tried six weeks ago to get Don to replace him." The new champion, Lennox Lewis, said, "At first, when he was walking away, I thought he was trying to trick me or something." At a news conference the day after the fight, McCall explained his crying by saying that he was trying to get himself into an emotional state.

In April 1997, he was detained in hospital after his wife took out an emergency custody order against him. Mental health experts confirmed that he was mentally ill and in need of hospitalization.

Remarkably, the 59 year-old McCall is still fighting, his last pro fight, his 76th, saw him knock-ut Stacey Frazier in Round 2 in Texas in November 2024.

After the Durvan debacle, Mike Barrett announced more big plans for me when he told reporters he'd fixed me up with a month's training in New York where I'd be coached by none other than Teddy Atlas, who had once worked with a teenage Mike Tyson. I'd been training with Arthur Urray, who'd replaced Bobby Neill after the Boucher defeat. But that wasn't working out because I didn't feel I was learning very much from him.

And, true to Mike's word, I spent an amazing month in New York with Atlas at Gleason's Gym in New York. Some of the biggest names in boxing had either trained there or were training there when I arrived. They included Chris Eubank, who was there at the same time as me, and Pernell Whitaker, who already held the IBF and WBC world lightweight titles. The atmosphere was amazing. They had four rings and they were always full. The sparring was vicious, as if they were trying to kill each other. They told me that if I wasn't good enough they'd kick me out after day one. I survived a month and I knew just being there for that short time had sharpened me up no end.

When I got back to the UK for the October showdown with Mickey Hughes I was in the best shape of my life and fired up. The fight was being billed as make or break for both of us. Hughes said on the day, "I'm confident but I know if I get beaten it's the end of the road for me."

My manager was displaying his usual pre-fight optimism saying, "I saw Gary at the weekend and I couldn't believe the improvement. He has all the fire needed to compete at the top level and I have no doubt he will be fighting for a world title before 1991 is out."

He couldn't have been more wrong.

From my perspective the night was an even bigger disaster than losing to Boucher or McGirt. I was the hot, odds-on favourite and, with Atlas in my corner, I dominated from the start and won the first five rounds with ease. I hit

Hughes so hard and often I don't know how he managed to stay alive, never mind in the fight. Then in the sixth there was an accidental clash of heads and a big cut opened up above my left eye. My vision was impaired but I continued to chase Hughes around the ring landing big punches from every angle. I'd won six of the first seven rounds comfortably and had lost only one. Then in the eighth Hughes landed one very lucky punch. It was a left hook to my jaw. It came out of nowhere and incredibly, for the first time in my 31-fight career, I was knocked out! I needed four stitches in my eye and it was decided I should go to hospital.

As ambulancemen wheeled me out of the arena, it was probably the most embarrassing moment of my career. At the hospital doctors decided to keep me in overnight for observation. Graham Sulkin was so worried about me he accompanied me to hospital and remained by my bedside until I was released the next morning.

We spoke for hours about the direction my career was going. We decided that it would probably be in my best interests if I split from Mike Barrett. Graham would take a hand in proceedings and help me get out of my contract. The plan was to get me signed up with Mickey Duff. In the meantime, Graham and his wife Jan invited me to move into their spacious home. It was a very generous offer and one which I had no trouble accepting.

I'd been very lucky with accommodation in London. I lived there for about ten years and never paid as much as a week's rent. I spent several years rent-free in a flat owned by Glasgow businessman Ivor Tiefenbrun, the electronics genius behind Linn Products. He had an empty flat in Swiss Cottage and wanted to help my career along. Then, when he needed the flat back, and I was in Glasgow, I was interviewed by Channel 4 for a documentary about boxing. During the few weeks I was involved I got to know and befriend Stuart Cosgrove who became head of Channel 4 in Scotland. At the time he was a senior producer.

One day we got chatting about London. I was planning to move back down there but had nowhere to stay. I asked him for some advice about finding the right property to rent etc, when out of the blue he offered me his own London flat, which was lying empty. Stuart insisted I stay there rent-free. His flat was in a nice part of Camden, but there was a rough housing estate nearby and there were plenty of break-ins on a regular basis.

Stuart had an enormous and valuable record collection in his flat and I know, back in Glasgow, he slept easier once I moved in. He reckoned anyone trying to break in while I was there would quickly regret it. He was probably spot-on but we never got the chance to find out because my time there was hassle free.

Soon I was on the move again. Living with the Sulkins allowed Graham and I to plot very carefully the next stage of my career. After the Hughes defeat it would be five months before my next fight. This would be the last time Mike Barrett would be in charge of my affairs.

Inevitably, perhaps, my manager and I parted on a subdued note. I was back in Glasgow at the Hospitality Inn on the undercard for Donnie Hood's International Bantamweight title defence against Vigilio Openio. No offence to either, but this was a new low for me after some of my recent escapades. My opponent in the eight-rounder on 5th March 1991 was one Kenny "The Tank" Louis from Mississippi.

Louis' record wasn't too bad, with 17 wins, seven losses and a draw on the tough American circuit. Despite that I gave him a bit of a tanking by knocking him out in the second.

Afterwards, Mike Barrett made the usual noises to the press about future title fights but by now we both knew it was all over between us. And it wasn't long before we went our separate ways. As usual in my life it wasn't a simple process. Barrett and Duff were no longer on speaking terms so there was no way they would discuss my contract. In the end Graham Sulkin bought my contract from Barrett for £35,000 and sold it to Mickey Duff for the same sum. It may have sounded like a lot of money for a fighter who was considered to be washed up, but Duff was no fool. He didn't get to become the dominant force in British boxing by making too many mistakes. He saw a great deal more potential in me than anyone else.

And he informed me in no uncertain terms that he expected me to prove him right!

A Fresh Start

MY NEW BOSS MOVED very quickly to get me back to the Royal Albert Hall and into the limelight. In doing so he displayed the kind of cautious approach I was used to under Maurice Lewis, who was remained in my corner.

I was on the undercard for Frank Bruno's comeback fight. Big Frank had been out for two years and nine months and some commentators described his return to the ring as crazy. He was financially set up for life and after two tough world title fights he had nothing left to prove. He was taking on John Emmen, who was best known for being a Dutch male model, although, coincidentally, he was one of only two men to have beaten Toyi Castro from Tenerife.

Mickey explained the match-up by saying, "Sure I've picked an opponent I think Frank can beat. I manage 32 fighters and never let any of them have fights I don't think they can win."

True to his word he had chosen an easy task for me, too, putting me in against Peter Eubank, older brother of my mate Chris, who was by now the WBO super-middleweight champ. Peter had a pretty poor record with just 14 wins and 20 losses to date. But he proved to be a bit more of a handful than anticipated, either that or I was still struggling to find form. There was no dubiety about my victory but, disappointingly, the fight went the distance, unlike big Frank's triumphant return which lasted just one round after the Dutchman was sent flying to the canvas three times.

As a professional boxer I, by and large, believed that my fate was always in my own fists. I had a simple philosophy: train as hard and as often as possible; be stronger than my opponent; inflict more pain on my opponent than he can on me by hitting him harder and more often than he can hit me but sometimes, on rare occasions, an event outwith my control could have a major influence on me. And that's exactly what happened on Friday 29th November 1991, just over a month after the Eubank fight.

Simon Brown, whom I'd seen triumph easily in Budapest two-and-a-half years earlier, was defending his WBC World Welterweight title against Buddy McGirt in Las Vegas. Prior to the fight I was asked by a journalist for my opinion on the outcome. "Brown will beat him," I responded.

Deep down I felt that was a bit of an understatement. I reckoned Brown, who had won nine title fights in a row, would destroy the man who beat me. But I was reluctant to say so in public in case it was seen as sour grapes. This more cautious approach was yet another clear sign that I was finally growing up. In my younger days I would have blurted out my feelings without regard for the consequences.

In the event McGirt dominated from the start and won a convincing unanimous points decision. Suddenly, much of the self-doubt that had cast a shadow of gloom over me after recent defeats disappeared. I began to see Buddy McGirt in a new light. No question, he was a true world champion. Yet, while relatively inexperienced, I had managed to go the distance with him.

What did that performance say about me? I knew the answer to that question immediately. I realised then that I was good enough to mix in these exalted circles, that I was good enough for a world title crack at the very least. My self-belief was back. I discovered a new-found confidence in my own abilities. Nothing was going to stop me now!

I went back to the gym with renewed vigour. I pounded the pavements longer and more often than before. Everyone who knew me saw a change in me from that moment on. And it wasn't long before the "new" Gary Jacobs was back in action.

On 21st February 1992, I topped the bill at a packed SECC

in Glasgow, taking on old foe Del Bryan for his British title. And even before a punch was thrown my manager was waxing lyrical about a victory for me opening the door for further glory. Mickey said, "I have honestly never seen him looking better in the gym and I'm confident he can win the title. There are many avenues for us to go down if Gary becomes champion. He could attempt to regain the Commonwealth title, but I would prefer to go for the IBF world championship held by American Maurice Blocker."

I was feeling good and I was confident of repeating my 1988 victory over Bryan but I knew that deeds, not words, were required. I told the press I thought I was the underdog, but other than that I kept my mouth shut. The champion, meanwhile, had plenty to say. Referring to my previous victory over him he stated, "I'm a different fighter now. I'm the man with the title and he's not getting it. I've a score to settle and another title win means I can keep the Lonsdale Belt."

The pre-fight pundits were divided on the outcome. Some pointed out that Bryan had won the title against Kirkland Laing then defended it successfully against Mickey Hughes - who had knocked me out. So that gave him the edge in their eyes. Quite simply I knew I had to win. If I lost, my career would probably never recover.

From the first bell I controlled the centre of the ring hitting the champ with everything I had. After 12 rounds I'd won six, lost three, with three drawn. It was a comprehensive triumph and I used the occasion to take a swipe at my detractors, telling the press, "I hope they are proud of themselves now, all those people who said two years ago that I was finished. They were basing that on my defeats to Buddy McGirt and Donovan Boucher. But what they conveniently forgot was that McGirt had already won one world title and went on to take another after beating me. Boucher is now high in the world ratings and has been rewarded for his achievements."

In the build-up to the fight one reporter had written,

"Scottish title holder at 21, Commonwealth Champion at 22 and winner of the WBC International crown at 23, sceptics say the best is behind Jacobs." Well, I was now 26 and British Champion.

Mickey Duff was ecstatic, saying, "I'm sending a cable and a tape of the fight to Butch Lewis, manager of IBF world champion Maurice Blocker, inviting him to defend against Gary. The earliest I could see this happening would be May and the Conference Centre in Glasgow assure me they can accommodate 8,500 fans for what would be a fantastic occasion."

I'd hardly had time to draw breath before I was back in action. Just over a month later, on 23rd March, I faced American Tommy Small at the Royal Albert Hall, one of the support bouts as Duke McKenzie tried to take a step closer to creating boxing history.

The wee man from Croydon had become the first Briton to hold world titles in two different divisions. He'd won the IBF Flyweight title in 1988 and the WBO Bantamweight crown in 1991. Chris Eubank had then equalled the feat, first by defeating WBO Middleweight champ Nigel Benn in November 1990, then, three months later by stopping Michael Watson in their ill-fated WBO Super-middleweight title clash. Now Duke was hoping to become the first to hold a world title in three weights. He wanted to add the Super-bantam belt to his collection and would succeed just over six months later, but first he had to dispose of tough Puerto Rican Wilfredo Vargas. In the event he did so with ease, stopping him in the eighth.

My fight was even quicker and easier. Small couldn't survive my big punches and lasted just 4 minutes 40 seconds of what was a scheduled 10-rounder. Small, from Virginia, had won 25 of his 29 fights but he was unable to cope with my aggression and was back-pedalling right from the start. He needed a count of eight after I connected with a beauty of a right hook at the start of the second round and couldn't

A Fresh Start

defend himself when I went in for the kill.

Fights were coming thick and fast now. Mickey had seen a change in me and was trying to strike while the iron was hot. So, a few weeks later I was back in the ring at Wembley Arena up against Mexican Nino Cirilo, while the defence of my British title against Welshman John Davies had already been agreed and this was supposed to be a warm-up. Cirilo wasn't expected to be as much of a pushover as Small. In his previous fight he went the distance against former world welterweight champion Aaron Davies. It was only his third defeat and he could boast 14 wins and 3 draws going in against me. I was quietly confident telling reporters, "Everything's going fine and I've never felt fitter." And, perhaps providing a clue about the matter consuming my everyday thoughts, I added: "I will get my world title chance as long as I keep winning."

Things turned out pretty much as expected. I won a convincing points decision after dominating for most of the ten rounds. The Davies fight was still five months away, scheduled for 9th July 1992, but after that my future was unclear. Suddenly all that changed when along came another of those life-altering events beyond my control. Once again Buddy McGirt played a starring role.

However, before that could take place an even more important date awaited me. The birth of my first child. Olivia arrived on Thursday 21st May 1992 at Rutherglen Maternity Hospital. I'm delighted to say I was there for the big occasion. Now this really was a life-changing event – and the joy it brought to my life has never ceased.

On 25th June, McGirt travelled to Italy to defend his WBC Welterweight crown against European champ Patrizio Oliva. The American beat the local hero with a unanimous points decision. On 7th July 1992, just two days prior to my title defence at the SECC, Oliva unexpectedly announced his retirement. All of a sudden I was being lined up to take on French champion Ludovic Proto for the vacant European crown. He was ranked as the number one challenger and I was at number two. Not only that, but Mickey was confident he'd get the fight to Glasgow by putting up a purse of £75,000.

First, though, I'd have to dispose of John Davies. What had been a straightforward British title defence had been transformed into a make-or-break battle. To complicate matters further, Davies had to pull out after cracking a rib while sparring. He was replaced by Robert Wright, who wasn't considered as dangerous. Out of the blue, the stakes had been raised beyond recognition. Lose to Wright and I would miss out on the Proto fight. Beat Wright and Proto and it would be almost impossible to deny me a world title shot.

There was great speculation about how the whole scenario would unfold. There was talk of me facing WBO champ Manning Galloway, although I made it clear I wanted a re-match with McGirt. Inside, I was highly-excited at the direction my career could soon take, but on the outside I was the king of cool.

"Don't worry I'll keep my title," I told reporters, "I know exactly what I have to do. I treat all my fights as world title shots, this one is no different. The change of opponent makes no difference either. Wright will have a rough time coming to my hometown and trying to take away the title I have worked so hard to get. I've got used to having the Lonsdale Belt by my side and I need to win twice more to keep it. A European title fight is just the incentive I need."

Into this maelstrom, Robert Wright arrived in Glasgow full of confidence. "I'll beat Jacobs," he said. "I'm a strong puncher and can win in any round."

The challenger probably convinced himself he stood a chance because two of his three defeats came at the hands of men who'd beaten me – Mickey Hughes and Donovan Boucher. It's possible he reckoned he and I were on a par, but Wright couldn't have been more wrong. He failed to realise that that was the old Gary Jacobs. Now he was facing the new, energised version and in my current mental and physical condition I would have beaten Hughes and Boucher, and that's exactly what I did to Mr Wright, who lasted just half of the scheduled 12 rounds. I knew beforehand that victory alone wasn't enough. I had to look good and win in style. And I did.

It was one of my best performances to date. I chose every delivery carefully, trying to make each one count and it all seemed to click into place. In the fourth round I landed two massive punches on his chin but he managed to weather the storm and come back at me. In the sixth and final round he couldn't defend himself as I hit him with a flurry of blows. As the ref shouted out the count Wright could be heard saying, "no more, man". He got his wish. Mickey was ecstatic and full of lavish praise telling the media, "That was the best I've ever seen him box."

Almost immediately Mickey set wheels in motion to bring the Proto showdown to Glasgow saying, "I have a history of giving Scots the chance to fight for titles at home - Chic Calderwood, Jim Watt, Peter Keenan - Gary is no different. I want to take him all the way."

I was also desperate for the fight to go ahead in my hometown. In the aftermath of the victory over Wright I told the media, "I have never seen Proto in action, even on video, but I am not concerned about what he can do. I know what I can do and so do the Glasgow fight fans. I just pray I get the chance to go for the European title in front of my own people." Unfortunately, Mickey didn't succeed and that led to what became yet another scandalous night for boxing.

The fight, which would severely tarnish the reputation of European boxing, was arranged for 16th October 1992 in Paris. Once again, the lack of interest shown by British TV was a decisive factor. It was different in France where Proto, with 24 straight wins and no losses, was one of their few boxing successes at the time and akin to a national hero. The 27-year-old from Guadeloupe in the Caribbean was a huge favourite with the fans and French broadcasters put up plenty of cash to ensure the showdown would stay in the French capital.

Mickey knew I was ready for Proto come the big day. I told everybody that I'd worked harder for this fight, the biggest for me yet, than any other and it was the truth. I would give it my best shot. I was confident because I had fought and won against a higher class of opponent than he had faced. But just to be sure I was focussed on the job, the night before the fight Mickey handed me another major incentive. At our Paris hotel he announced that if I won I might soon be challenging for the world title in Glasgow. He told the assembled journalists, "Gary has a good chance of pulling it off. If he does then he could be lined up to face IBF champ Maurice Blocker in Glasgow early in the new year. I'm a great believer in getting home ground for my fighters."

But first up was Monsieur Proto.

I was taking him very seriously indeed and it was a bit of a compliment to him that in my build-up I had sparred more rounds than for any other previous opponent.

When one reporter reminded me that no Scot had ever won a boxing title in France, and that the last to try failed way back in 1919, I responded, "There is a first time for everything. Proto is tall, just like my last opponent, Robert Wright, whom I destroyed with uppercuts on the inside. I know I've got to do the same with Proto." And, perhaps prophetically, I added, "I just don't trust European judges."

The fight went according to plan, my plan! I easily won the first six rounds and after that he came more into it. But even being generous to my opponent I was at least a couple of rounds ahead at the end. Yet two of the judges awarded him the victory.

I was furious, although not totally surprised. I knew that if Proto was still standing at the end then my chances of winning would be slim. Such is boxing life for most Brits on

Top: Maurice and I celebrate in the dressing room after beating Dave Douglas to win the Scottish title. I haven't a mark on me!

Below: Posters promoting both fights.

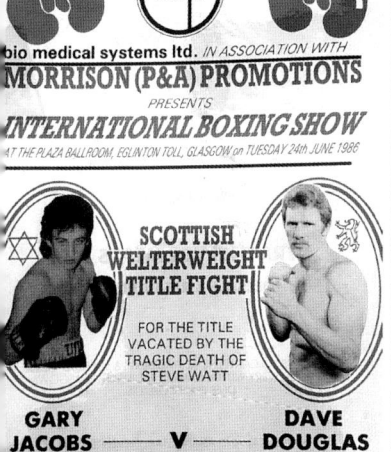

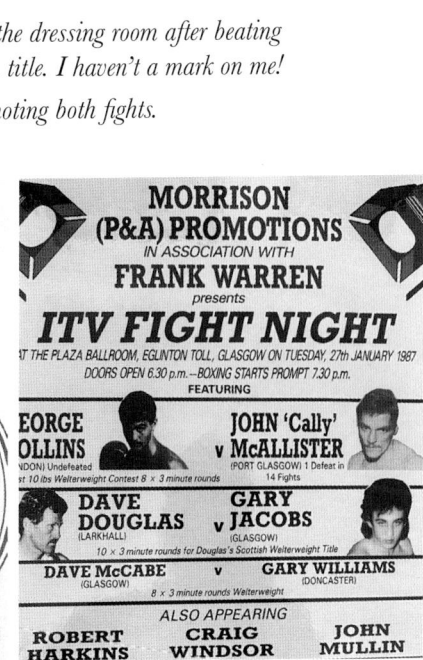

Maurice's letter requesting a re-match after my controversial defeat.

> **Maurice Lewis**
> BOXERS MANAGER and BOXING COACH
> (Licensed B.B.B.C.)
>
> Telephone 041 - 649 7629
>
> 15 DUDLEY COURT,
> LETHINGTON AVENUE,
> GLASGOW, G41
>
> SCOTTISH AREA Council 25/9/86.
>
> Dear Sir,
> I wish to put forward my boxer Gary Jacobs to challenge for the Scottish Welterweight Title. I feel that this is merited due to the controversial outcome of that contest in June 86. when he boxed Dave Douglas. at the Plaza Ballroom. June 86

For winning the Douglas fight I was awarded the Steve Watt Memorial Belt, a proud moment.

Celebrating with Bobby Neil after beating Wilf Gentzen.

With Scotland's Player of the Year, Celtic's Paul McStay.

With Mike Barrett when things were going well between us.

Here I am celebrating after a well-deserved Vegas victory over Suazo..

No TV!

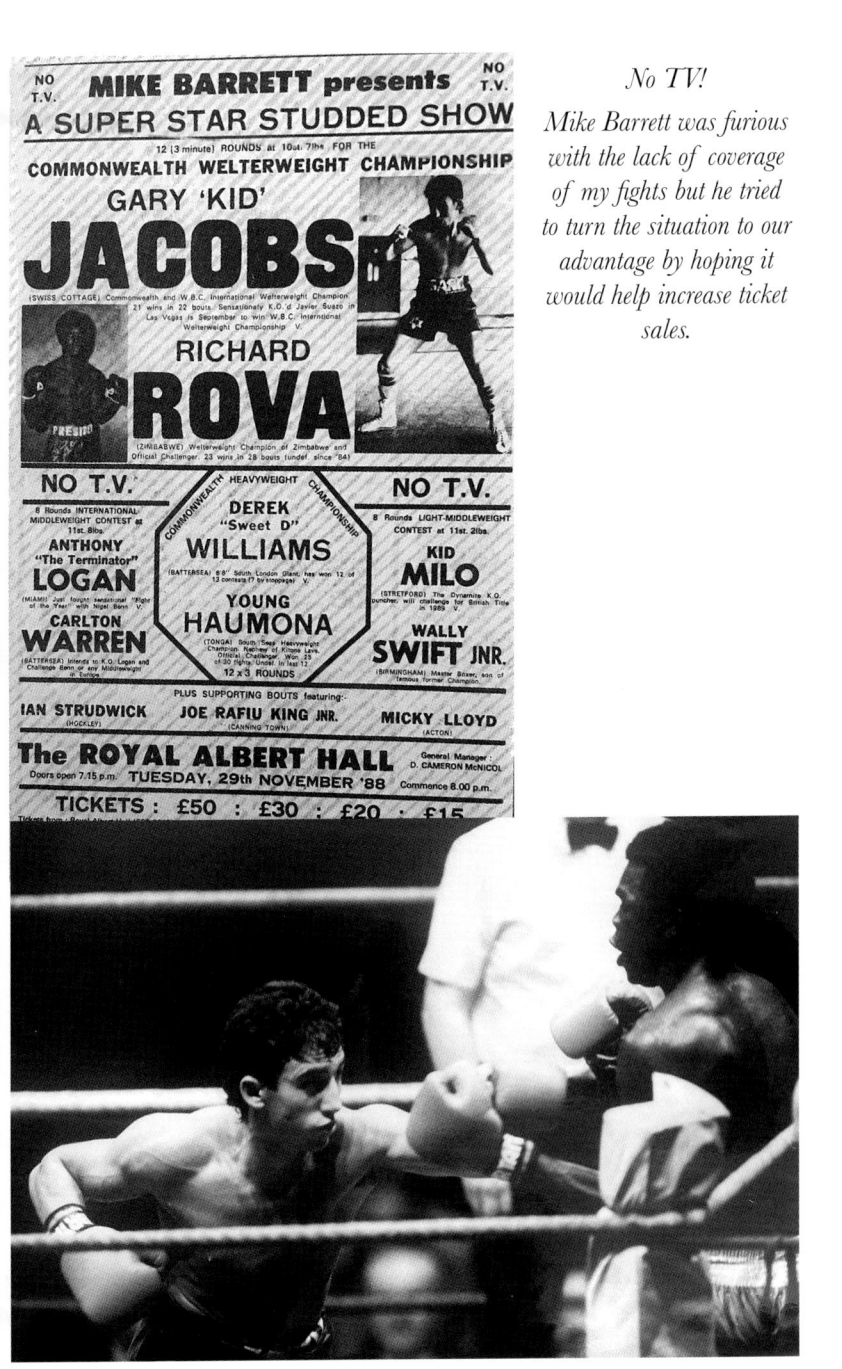

Mike Barrett was furious with the lack of coverage of my fights but he tried to turn the situation to our advantage by hoping it would help increase ticket sales.

Putting the pressure on Richard Rova.

Training with Bobby Neil.

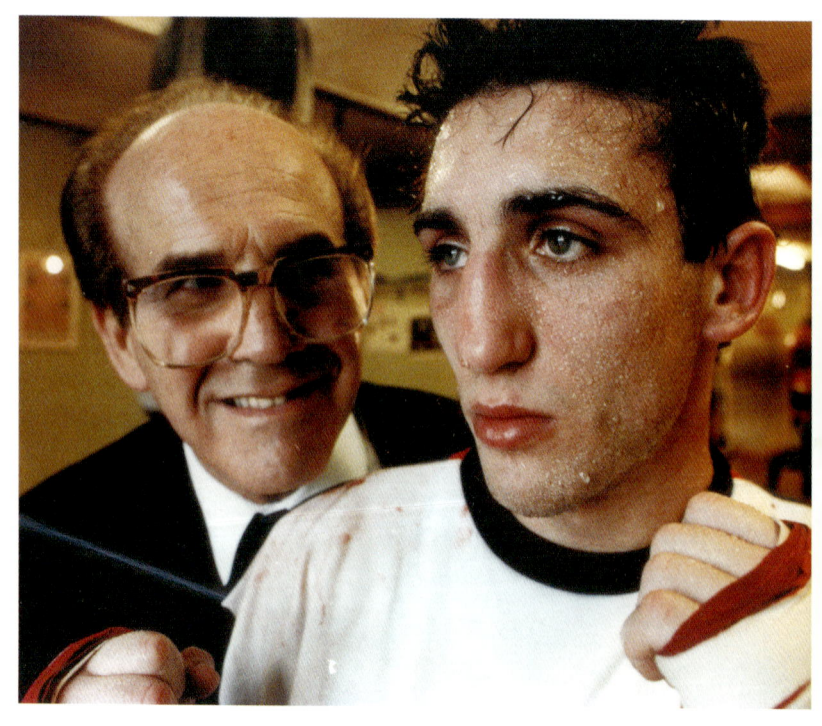

Legendary promoter Mickey Duff and I shortly after he bought out my contract from Mike Barrett.

Turning on the power and style against a battered and bloodied Proto.

Maurice and I show our delight after beating Proto.

Finally wearing the coveted European Championship belt after taking it from Proto, although it should have been mine in the first place!

I had a thing about motorbikes and because of that Channel 4 asked Ewan McGregor and I to tour the West Highlands on bikes for a documentary. The producer was Stuart Cosgrove who now presents BBC Radio Scotland's Off the Ball *show.*

Maurice was a hard task-master, as his diary records show. I had been under his management for nearly a year and he was far from satisfied.

1983 October week 43

Mon 24 United Nations Day, Labour Day, New Zealand
light training
EASTERHOUSE.

Tue 25
MUST RUN

Wed 26
MISSED Training.

Thu 27
MUST RUN
…all off.

My complete and slightly underwhelming amateur career, as listed in my Western District Amateur Boxing Association Boxer's Record card.

Date	Tournament	Opponent	Duration	Decision	Remarks	M.O.	O.I.C.
30.11.82	CES	S HOOD	3x1	WON	(U)		
16.12.82	Scot Nat	I MURRAY	5x2	WON	RSC 2nd		
21.1.83	Scot Nat	D HAZLETT	3x1½	WON	KO 1ST		
12.2.83	CES	J HUGHES	3x2	WON	KO 2		
25.3.83	Scot Nat	G. RAE	3x2	WON	(U)		
29.4.83	Scot Nat	M. GINLEY	3x2	WON	KO 1		
7.10.83	CES	D DAVIDSON	3x2	LOST	P.		
21.10.83	Scot Nat	D MOSLEY	3x2	WON	RSC 2		
.11.83	BELLA++	R JEFFREY	3x2	WON	RET. 1		
29.11.83	WD CHAMPS	H. MULLEN	3x2	LOST	Pts		
27/2/84	SCES	D DAVIDSON	3x2	LOST	Pts (MAJ.)		
29/6/84	CLYDEVIEW	C. RAE	3x2	WON	UNAM		
20.11.84	W.D. CHAMPS	J. DEMPSEY	3x2	W.P	(UN)		
1/4/85	SCOT NAT	J LITTLE	3x2	LOST			

trained hard. but poor sparring

L-R My pal Pete Rose with Howard Jacob, my boss at the jewellery business.

With Maurice celebrating another triumph

Piling on the pressure against Tek Nkalankete during a defence of my European crown. I put him down within 30 seconds of the first round but he got up and held on for 12 rounds.

Maurice and I enjoy the atmosphere in Atlantic City before my training intensifies ahead of the World Title fight with Pernell Whittaker.

At the weigh-in for the Whitaker fight.

A group of friends came to Atlantic City to support me against Pernell Whitaker.

On the day of the fight they gave the locals a wee taste of Tartan.

Fight night was also kilt night in Atlantic City.

Entering the ring for the world title clash against Pernell Whitaker, with Maurice behind me and Mickey on the right. Just outside the ring is Tom Fitzsimmons, one of my pals who'd travelled from Scotland to support me.

Landing a blow on the Champ.

Top: Warming up with Martin Harkin prior to his European title fight against Liam Taylor in Bolton.

Bottom: Giving instructions to Martin during the bout.

the Continent. Despite that I thought I had dominated so conclusively that even partisan judges would be embarrassed to rule against me. The fact that Proto thought he'd lost made the result all the more difficult to take. As we awaited the verdict he leaned through the ropes and gave French journalists the thumbs down sign. And when his triumph was announced many locals in the crowd began booing and jeering. It was a blatant home-town decision. One judge, a Spaniard, had me losing by five rounds. The guy must have been watching another fight on another planet.

I knew I had fought well and quite simply I had been cheated out of the title. Mickey said, "It was disgraceful. Gary was robbed, he won the fight clearly. But that often happens on the Continent."

One sportswriter came up with an intriguing conspiracy theory about the reason for this particular blatant miscarriage of justice. Before the fight he predicted I might lose because Nigel Benn had a recent easy victory over an Italian. He wrote, "British Champion Gary Jacobs faces a Nigel Benn backlash when he bids to win the European title next week. He'll find all of Europe seething at the way Benn forced Mauro Galvano to retire after just three rounds in Italy last week to carry off the WBC Super Middleweight Crown. Anti-British feeling is running high after that result. Even though Jacobs will try to make it clear he is a Scot, he could be the first British boxer to catch the backlash. It's hard enough to win a title abroad for any but the bravest of Brits and Jacobs may find the task beyond him, given the present anti-Union Jack jingoism on the Continent."

Whatever the reason for one of boxing's most outrageous verdicts, the European Boxing Union showed their displeasure by ordering an immediate re-match. Jacobs v Proto II was arranged for 6th February 1993. I vowed that this time the judges wouldn't need to make a choice. The result would not be in doubt. I was going to take care of things myself, in my own way. I knew that if I didn't knock out my opponent there was a strong chance the decision would go his way again, even if I was the better fighter. So I had to finish him off.

This time I was also hoping for more vocal support from the crowd. I'd publicly appealed to Scottish fans in Paris for a rugby international to come to the fight and cheer me on. I knew quite a few had responded. On the night I was pretty hyped up because I was still so angry at the way the first fight turned out. Just before we left the changing room Maurice took me aside for a quiet word. I thought he was going to try to calm me down. That was his usual style ... but not this time. This time he wanted to wind me up!

We were fighting in the Circe d'Hiver in Paris. Maurice explained that he'd been studying the venue's history and he'd discovered that the Winter Circus, as it was known in English, was the final staging post for the French Jews who were sent by the Nazis to be massacred in the death camps. He told me all this and pleaded with me to fight for their memory. I can still remember his parting shot. "Gary, son, make sure that the Jews don't lose again in this awful place. Make sure they leave here tonight with their heads held high."

Well, if I was fired up beforehand this took me to the edge. Quite simply I was going to unleash the forces of history on my opponent and to be honest, at that point I didn't really care who that opponent was. It happened to be Ludovic Proto across the ring. It wasn't his fault. He personally hadn't done anything wrong, it was just his bad luck to be in the wrong place at the wrong time.

I took control right from the start. I knew Proto didn't have a knock-out punch so there was little for me to worry about. By the second round he was floored and bleeding heavily from a gash above his right eye after a devastating left hook. In the fifth round the ref, worried about the high level of punishment Proto was taking, called for the ringside doctor to examine him. The doc allowed him to fight on. I wasn't bothered one way or the other but I thought it was the wrong decision Proto had suffered badly and had lost a great deal of blood.

In the lovely home shared by Maurice and his wife, Rosemary, there is a massive, framed photo of the fight hanging in the hallway which illustrates the point. In the picture, Proto's trunks are coloured pink. At the start of the fight they were white. The change was caused by the torrent of blood from his eye.

In the seventh I struck with a flurry of heavy hits to his battered body. Proto was now hanging on as best he could, with little or no hope of retrieving the situation. In the eighth I hit him 27 times without reply before a couple of solid left hooks had him almost down and out but, propped up by the ropes, he survived until the bell intervened on his behalf. It was all over within 15 seconds of the start of the ninth. I landed two vicious lefts and the Frenchman collapsed in a heap onto the floor. His corner immediately threw in the towel to stop the fight and save their man from further disaster. As I celebrated winning the Euro crown, Maurice climbed into the ring, gave me a wee smile and nodded. It was mission accomplished in more ways than one.

My Mentor

ON THE WAY HOME from Paris, I spent a great deal of time reflecting on the journey Maurice and I had taken together so far. When we had first met, Maurice Lewis couldn't possibly have known it at the time, but he and I had just taken the first tentative step on a journey towards a destination beyond our wildest dreams. Unlike me, he had plenty of dreams. In fact, until I turned up at his door that night, that's about all he had. And I'm not being disrespectful to him when I say that.

And yet, within a few short years the dreams would come true in spectacular style. Maurice would find himself meeting and greeting some of boxing's biggest and brightest stars: Bob Arum, Mike Barrett, Mickey Duff, Chris Eubank, Frank Bruno, Teddy Atlas and the incomparable Don King were just a few of the legends with whom he'd rub shoulders. It was a remarkable turnaround in a career which, hitherto, had been anything but remarkable.

Maurice was a jeweller and watchmaker who owned a small business, but his obsession was boxing. He'd first fallen in love with the fight game as a teenager and had subsequently spent the best part of his lifetime talking and thinking about it. He was a deep thinker and keen observer of the sweet science. He was intelligent, well-read and shrewd. He also possessed a great sense of humour, which would serve him well as he helped guide my career from obscurity to fame and fortune.

He'd developed many great ideas and strategies which he felt would be successful in the ring. Certainly, he was convinced they were great. There was a problem, however. Until I made a surprise entrance into his life, Maurice was a minor figure operating on the outer fringes of the sport. He'd been languishing in the bargain basement of Scottish boxing for many years and there were no signs of him ever entering the spotlight.

Maurice was a bit part player, helping a Glasgow trainer who ran a string of amateurs, most of whom weren't even promising. But he dreamed of the big time. And, clearly, he had potential, although not even he, in his wildest imagination, could envisage he'd fulfil it so impressively.

Maurice saw himself as a trainer or manager, but he didn't have anyone to train or manage. He spent much of his spare time hanging around with Jimmy Murray, who was responsible for guiding the early career of a young Jim Watt. Maurice helped in Jimmy's gym, took care of some admin work, helped sell tickets for shows and was occasionally allowed to pitch in with some training ideas. He was unpaid and unrecognised. Indeed many years later Jim Watt would say, "I don't remember much about him. I think he once maybe drove me to a training session in Kilmarnock."

Yet Maurice knew his boxing. And he knew and understood far more in those early unsung days than anyone ever gave him credit for.

"My husband was waiting for an opportunity to put his theories into practice and you, Gary, gave that to him," said his widow Rosemary. "Outside his family, the love of his life was boxing and he got that from an early age thanks to a piece of creative thinking by his father. Maurice's father, Sammy, was a barber who had a shop at Anderston Cross, not far from the centre of Glasgow. The family lived nearby in a tenement flat. It was a poor area with high unemployment. The shop was called Sammy Vessa's. He'd bought it from the Vessa family who were popular, well-known barbers in Glasgow and he had kept their name because he thought it would be good for trade. His real name was Sammy Pogalewitz. He'd been born in Holland but brought up in Belgium. His mother's family had been Dutch for centuries but his father was from Russia.

During the war he got called up by three different armies – the Dutch, Russian and British! They all sent papers for him but of course he fought for Britain.

"After the war, in the 1950s, it was really difficult to earn money as a barber. So to boost business he used to do the open razor shave with hot towels and some days he'd be very busy and that led to a problem. It was the older generation who would turn up for the open razor shave, which was more lucrative for Sammy. But if they saw a group of young men hanging around for a haircut they would go elsewhere. Some were possibly worried that the youngsters would cause trouble. Others just couldn't be bothered to wait in the queue. So Sammy came up with an ingenious solution. It kept the youngsters occupied and ensured the best paying customers didn't go elsewhere. The premises were very big so he built a full-size boxing ring in the back of the shop," revealed Rosemary.

"He then encouraged all the young men who would normally be milling around out front to get in the ring and box while they waited their turn for a haircut. It worked brilliantly. It was a win-win-win situation. The young men really enjoyed the boxing, especially since it didn't cost them anything and they were able to knock lumps out of each other. The older men were more relaxed about waiting in the queue without the young hotheads, and Maurice's father became busier and busier. If he tried that nowadays he'd be closed down by Health and Safety. But no-one ever got hurt in the back of Sammy's barber shop.

"Maurice, who was a teenager at the time, would work in the shop after school every day. He'd do a bit of brushing up the floor for his dad then he would jump into the ring and have a few rounds. Maurice didn't feel that he was particularly good at boxing, but he fell in love with it and often said he learned about strategies in the barber shop boxing ring."

As he grew into adulthood, Maurice spent more and more

time at boxing shows in and around Glasgow. He would often go with his best pal. Both saw themselves as worldly-wise, cool young men about town and it wasn't long before they got up to mischief together. His pal's name was Lewis Morris. For a laugh one day Maurice shortened his second name from Pogalewitz to Lewis and from that point on became officially known as Maurice Lewis. The happy-go-lucky pair would use the confusion caused by their names to their advantage.

One day Maurice was due to appear in court charged with a driving offence, so Lewis turned up and claimed he'd been wrongly accused. The sheriff had no option but to let him go, much to the bemusement of the arresting officers, who were seen leaving the court scratching their heads.

Then, in the mid 1960s, Maurice met and befriended Jimmy Murray, who was a well-known and respected Glasgow boxing trainer and manager. Murray ran a stable of fighters and owned his own small gym near the Kelvingrove Art Gallery. His most promising protege at the time was a teenage Jim Watt. Murray was very protective of Watt and wouldn't let anyone else get too close to him. However, he didn't have a car and Maurice did, so Maurice became Jimmy's unofficial chauffeur. Their friendship blossomed and before long Maurice would be found in the gym around two to three times a week.

Murray used to promote his own shows in places like Govan Town Hall. Maurice would help out with tickets and often acted as a cornerman when the fights got underway. This was the first chance Maurice got to put his ideas about boxing into practice and he enjoyed a small degree of success. One boxer in Murray's stable, heavyweight Davie Summers, wouldn't enter the ring unless Maurice was in his corner, sponging him down between rounds, dispensing advice and dealing with cuts. Davie looked on Maurice as his guardian angel.

As the friendship between Maurice and Jimmy deepened, Maurice and Rosemary's Shawlands flat became a regular hang-out for Murray and his entourage of fighters.

"Jimmy Murray was regarded by most of his boxers as more than just a trainer or manager," recalls Rosemary. "They looked upon him as more of a guru who dispensed wisdom. Most Saturday afternoons Murray and a few of them would congregate in our front room and Jimmy would hold court." Yet that was the depth of Maurice's involvement in the fight game, until I showed up.

The night after that first meeting between us Maurice drove me to the Govan Boxing Club. We entered a gym full of young men working out. Maurice directed me to an old punch bag hanging from the ceiling and demonstrated a few moves before asking me to have a go. To say I took to it like a duck to water would be a huge understatement. The noise, the smell and the atmosphere made me feel right at home from the very start. I wasn't too happy, though, when Maurice handed me a skipping rope. I asked him, 'what the fuck is this for?' Maurice, who was always quietly spoken, just told me to get on with it.

Although he was small of stature and a bit on the fat side, Maurice had an air of authority which demanded respect. So I just did what I was told and never answered back. Maurice was testing me that night and liked what he saw.

He later admitted, "Gary was an extremely gifted footballer and might have made the grade as a pro. But that was not to be. He joined in on the boxing training and loved it and I soon discovered he could carry a heavy clout in his fists."

By the time I met him Maurice had lost his business, a jewellery shop in Shawlands, but was able to make a decent living selling gems to a small group of private clients. Without premises to worry about his working arrangements were more flexible and he was able to devote plenty of time to boxing and, as he concentrated more and more of his efforts on me, Maurice's 15-year friendship with Jimmy Murray began to dissolve.

Maurice's first step was to register me with the Western District of the Scottish Amateur Boxing Association. This he did on 19th October 1982. I was now a fully signed-up member of the Govan Amateur Boxing Club, fighting in the welterweight (10 stone 7 pound) division.

At the same time Maurice put a training plan into action. I was naturally right-handed but he was determined to turn me into a southpaw. It was his first priority. Maurice knew that orthodox right-handed boxers struggled against left-handed opponents and was determined to give me every possible advantage. From day one he insisted I learned to jab with my right and power in with my left. It felt a bit strange at first but I soon got used to it.

The other thing Maurice insisted on doing was taking me to different gyms so I could experience an array of sparring partners, each of whom had their own style. The constant variation taught me early on how to cope with all sorts of different tactics and techniques. Within seven weeks of entering a boxing gym for the first time I was ready for my first fight. It was an unforgettable day because nothing really went to plan.

Maurice's diary entry for that day is simple and to the point: "30th November 1982, Palace of Arts. Jacobs v Hood. Three one-minute rounds. Won points, unanimous. Raw but determined."

However, my recollections are much more vivid.

The fight took place at the Palace of Arts in Bellahouston Park. There were 27 fights on the card and I was last. At one point I'd been waiting so long I was starving so I wolfed down a fish supper. Hardly the ideal preparation! When the bell went all the technique and training I'd learned went out the window. I was nervous and terrified. I ran across the ring arms flailing and head down. There were only two things on my mind: I didn't want to get hurt and I didn't want to lose, especially since my dad was watching.

Just over two weeks later, on 16th December, I was back in action. This time I triumphed much more easily, but Maurice, always a hard task-master, was not happy. To this day I don't understand why he felt that way. I absolutely hammered my opponent, yet Maurice wrote in his diary, "Fairfield Social Club Govan, Jacobs v Murrell, three two-minute rounds. Won, referee stopped contest in first round after right hands to body and head. Must be more controlled and accurate."

At the start of 1983 Maurice started taking me training three times a week. The venue alternated between the Govan club, Kelvin club (Govanhill) and the Blantyre club. The last of these was run by former Commonwealth Games gold medallist John McDermott who would go on to play a major role in my professional career. By 14th January Maurice was beginning to see good progress. His diary was peppered with comments like, "Looking well," and "Looks good."

A week later I was back in the ring and Maurice couldn't have been more pleased with the display. The diary states: "Civic Centre Motherwell, Jacobs v Haslett. Won KO first. Very efficient win was on target instantly." The last word was underlined twice. But if Maurice thought that I had found some level of consistency he was in for a disappointment. I fought a chap called Hughes in the Easterhouse Community Centre on 12th February. I knocked him out in the second round. Maurice noted, "Poor first round, poor defence. Complete transformation second round." I won my next fight, on 25th March at Paisley Town Hall, but Maurice was growing more concerned. After three two-minute rounds against 'G. Rae' I was awarded a unanimous decision. However, the diary entry revealed a note of extreme caution. "Must improve boxing technique before further contests to avoid unnecessary punishment."

It was at this point that Maurice decided it was time for me to take time off from training. The short break seemed to work wonders. I returned to the gym with great zeal and my efforts began to pay off. My sixth fight was on 28th April at Fairfield Social Club. Maurice was delighted as McGinley was knocked out in the first round. "Tremendous power in evidence," he wrote, "must guard against over-confidence." Unfortunately, I didn't get the opportunity to build on that great display. It would be more than five months before my next fight. It would turn out to be the toughest of my short career so far.

There were no clues in the lead-up to the bout that anything might go wrong. On Wednesday 14th September Maurice's diary entry stated, "Paisley Club, three two-minute sparring rounds with Dave Haggerty. Starting to look like a pro." Five days later Maurice wrote, "Five rounds sparring (Hughes, McGinley, Dyer) handled them all confidently." At the same time, across town, in the East End of Glasgow, two people were quietly and methodically plotting my downfall. Bobby Keddie had enjoyed a prolific amateur boxing career and continued to represent Scotland while in his late 30s. He became a highly-respected trainer. One of his boxers was a classy welterweight called Davie Davidson, who was lined up to face me on Saturday 1st October 1983 at the Easterhouse Social Club. It was a day I will never forget. I suffered my first defeat when a points decision went against me after three two-minute rounds. Maurice had no complaints. He commented, "High-class opposition. Gary was against a very skilful opponent and was unable to land cleanly. If he had been able to maintain pressure would have won. Will be top class if he can build up lung power to sustain attacks."

Four months later, in the re-match, Davidson beat me again. I had no complaints either time. Davie was just too good for me at that stage of my career. He also had, in Bobby Keddie, a brilliant strategist. Keddie, who died in February 2015 aged 76, wasn't surprised by these results. He'd been working with Davidson for two years and knew his strengths. More importantly, he knew all about my strengths. "When Davie first came to me he was a fat boy, really flabby and at least a stone and a half overweight," he recalled years later, "but even then I saw he had potential so I spent 18 months getting his weight down and working on his fitness. Only then did I start teaching him proper boxing techniques. He became a lovely boxer but he had no punch. Davie could hit you all night without putting you down. But Gary could bang. We knew he would come at Davie bobbing and weaving and he was a hard hitter even in those days. So I taught Davie to get in close, land a couple of quick punches then get out of range again before Gary could unload the big guns. Gary wouldn't take you out with one punch but if he hit you, he would really hurt you. Davie was a smart boy and he kept his wits about him both times. He followed the instructions from the corner to the letter - jab and move, jab and move."

Davidson's lack of a big punch put paid to any dreams he may have had of becoming a professional fighter, but Bobby Keddie, like many others in the close-knit West of Scotland boxing scene, could see I was destined for greater things, even if I couldn't. I knew, especially after these two defeats, that I still had a lot to learn as an amateur and Maurice, shrewdly, fixed me up with another fight just 20 days after that first defeat.

In between he worked on my fitness by increasing the duration and frequency of my training runs. And on Friday 21st October I bounced back with an easy victory. Jacobs v Dempsey at Johnstone Town Hall was stopped by the referee in the second round. Maurice wrote, "Good win, extra fitness was crucial."

Yet all was not sweetness and light in our relationship. Within three days of the Dempsey fight Maurice was angrily writing in diary, "MUST RUN. MUST RUN. Unless Gary runs will call off next fight." The message got through to me, and I started running home from Govan to Shawlands after gruelling training sessions which included several rounds of sparring.

A fortnight later, on Thursday 3rd November, I was back in action in the Bellahouston Hotel and again emerged with an easy victory. 'R. Jeffrey' was described by Maurice as a "fast and competent boxer". However, he retired hurt in the first round. Maurice commented, "Gary looked really sharp and determined."

Despite those encouraging words my career appeared to take one step forward and two back. Throughout the following week Maurice was concerned about the poor standard of sparring in my training sessions, and when I took to the ring again, on Tuesday 22nd November, in the Western District Championships I lost on points to Harry Mullen. For the first time in my career, I failed to make the 67-kilo weight limit. I was forced to skip for 20 minutes before succeeding at the second attempt and that took too much out of me. After the fight it was discovered I had another problem, a poisoned foot. I was out for the rest of the year.

Meanwhile, Maurice had used his connections in the jewellery trade to find me a job. I started in a city-centre workshop learning how to carry out repairs to rings, chains and necklaces. The owner of the business was called Howard Jacob, which often led to a bit of confusion. Alongside me, also learning the ropes, worked a young chap called Peter Rose and we soon became great friends. In his heyday Peter's father, Syd, was Scotland's biggest independent jewellery retailer. He owned seven busy shops in prime sites in the centre of Glasgow and Edinburgh. Howard Jacob got the bulk of Syd's repair work and one of my jobs was picking up the gems from the shops and returning them once they'd been sorted. It meant I frequently wandered about the city centre with jewellery worth tens of thousands of pounds in my pockets.

Maurice used to tell people he wanted me to learn a trade so that I could fall back on something if the boxing didn't work out. Looking back it became clear to me I was hired because

I could look after myself in a dangerous situation. Apart from a wage, there were other benefits with being associated with these people. Syd became my first sponsor, paying for gloves, shorts and other training items. By the time I made my comeback I had turned 18, but it was no triumphant return. On 25th February 1984, at the Centaur pub in Easterhouse, Davie Davidson became the only man to defeat me twice. Next came two more victories against opponents I'd already beaten, Rae and Dempsey, before I finally kissed good-bye to my amateur gloves on 4th April 1985 against 'J. Little'. Like the majority of my bouts to date it consisted of three, two-minute rounds. I lost but it really didn't matter to me or anyone in my camp. Maurice didn't even record the details in his diary. He had more important things on his mind. I was turning pro, and that process, like so much in my life, was far from smooth. In fact, it might never have happened.

A highly-successful amateur career does not guarantee glittering prizes as a pro. And making the transition from one to the other is not a straightforward affair. My amateur record of eight victories and four defeats was unimpressive on two counts: it wasn't a great win ratio and in some quarters it was felt the relatively small number of fights did not provide me with adequate experience and grounding for what would lie ahead. There was, therefore, strong opposition against granting me a pro licence.

John McDermott, who won every domestic amateur title going, including featherweight gold at the 1962 Commonwealth Games in Perth, Australia, was unenthusiastic about my professional prospects. John, who ran a thriving boxing club at the Blantyre Miners' Welfare Club, was called on by Maurice to help with my amateur training from time to time and knew me well. He recalled, "Maurice would bring Gary to Blantyre for sparring and in those days he didn't look anything out of the ordinary. He was strong, fit and he trained well but he wasn't a particularly skilful boxer. I reckon, from memory, there were a number of younger boys in our gym who were more stylish and had better technique. I also felt Gary hadn't had enough bouts to justify turning professional. If you look at some of the top Scottish fighters, like world title holders Jim Watt and Ken Buchanan, they had distinguished and lengthy amateur careers. Both won the British Amateur title before turning pro."

Maurice took the opposite view. He believed that if I stayed an amateur for much longer, I would settle into a comfort zone and get used to three two-minute rounds. He had lofty ambitions for me and was desperate to realise them as soon as possible.

Bobby Keddie, who had 300 amateur fights at welterweight and lost only 13, sympathised with both points of view but on balance he agreed with Maurice at the time. "John's right when he says a good amateur career can set you up to become a good professional," he said, "but it's hard to get rid of bad habits once they're established. It's much easier to prevent them in the first place. Personally, I don't want a boy to box too much at amateur level, because if he's good he'll be picked for his country. And when you fight against other countries you're not fighting another boxer, you're fighting the best boxer in that country. They'll be good fighters who may have been at the European Championships. You're up against top dogs who'll give you hard fights. These take a lot out of you and can reduce the length of your career. If you're out of your depth early on and take punishment it can sicken you.

"You don't learn by fighting mugs. At the same time you don't learn by fighting good guys who can hit hard too early in your career. You've got to build up slowly. Nowadays turning pro early is quite common, mainly because there isn't a great deal of amateur opposition available. In terms of the optimum number of amateur fights, it depends on the individual boy. Some are ready after 12 fights and some might not be.

"Gary was full of confidence and enjoyed fighting. He would have fought anybody, anywhere, anytime. Plus he was clever, he never took many punches and had an awkward style which made him difficult to beat. He was ready."

Yet, unlike Bobby Keddie, John McDermott, as a member of the British Boxing Board of Control's committee which would consider my application to join the pro ranks, was in a position to influence my career. "When it came to the vote I voted against," he admits. "Luckily for Gary the majority round the table disagreed with me and he got his licence."

In view of what was to follow in my life, in and out the ring, this was a pivotal moment. Had John been more persuasive I would have been forced to pursue a different career path. I was already fed up with the amateur scene, mainly because I needed to earn a living. I often reflect on that vote and the discussions round the table and I still feel uneasy about a system which allows other people to have so much control over my affairs. Everything would have been different had my application been rejected. Yet, it was all down to a matter of opinion. There was nothing scientific or logical about it.

However, there's no time for grudges in boxing. Maurice had developed a huge amount of respect for McDermott and despite his vote of no confidence, he immediately approached him to become my full-time professional trainer. This freed Maurice to concentrate on management, particularly choosing the right opponents for me. This was a crucial element in plotting my progress. Maurice understood the psychology of boxing and could see I was worried about making the leap from amateur to pro, especially the step up from three two-minute rounds to six three-minute rounds. Although for the first few fights the rounds would last just two minutes.

In addition, he knew that no matter how confident I had been when taking on amateurs, there would be doubts about my own ability lurking in the back of my mind at the start of a new career. These doubts would last for many years and would only disappear after I had suffered a comprehensive defeat at the hands of one of the world's top fighters.

I was embarking on a whole new career, which requires new skills and thinking. Yet Maurice wasn't the only one doing the thinking. The day I turned pro I decided to live and act like a pro.

From that moment on I trained twice a day, five days a week. Although I never drank, I smoked the odd cigarette while still an amateur, I stopped that altogether. I knew that hard training was the key to success. If I was fitter and stronger than the other guy I would have a better chance of winning and avoid getting badly hurt.

Fighting professionally was a painful experience even when I won. You get hit harder and more often as a pro and I would always take a week off to recover after a fight. So it was Maurice's job to find opponents who wouldn't inflict too much damage on me while I learned the business. And the first of these was Mike Joyce, a 25-year-old who'd been born in Livingston but was now based in Doncaster. He had lost his first three fights and was considered suitable cannon fodder, but 24 hours before the fight Joyce pulled out and he was replaced by John Conlan, a Liverpudlian who was also making his pro debut that night and was, therefore, an unknown quantity.

This was a risky contest for me but there was no other option because of the time factor. Maurice's carefully laid plans were in tatters. He was very worried but I was unconcerned. I was looking forward to picking up my first pay packet, £100, and I didn't care who I had to hit to get it.

For that debut pro bout, at The Hospitality Inn, Glasgow on 20th May 1985, I was bottom of the bill on a show arranged by The Whitbread Scotland Sporting Club. It went the distance and at the end of six rounds I was the winner on points by Glaswegian referee Len Mullen. Just over 18 months later he would feature in one of the most controversial ring decisions of my career. Maurice needn't have worried unduly about Conlan. His career lasted less than 18 months and just six fights. When he retired he'd won three and lost three. It wasn't impressive but it was much better than Joyce's final record of no wins and four defeats.

Prior to the fight much was made of my Jewish background. One newspaper wrote, "The Shawlands teenager will be the first Glasgow-based Jewish fighter to box in the city since the days of Vic Herman who fought Peter Keenan in 1950. Herman was a battler and Jacobs is in the same mould." On the night the programme included the following message from promoters Eddie Coakley and Matt Sawers, "We would also like to take this opportunity in introducing Gary Jacobs, the first Jewish-born Glasgow boxer for over 20 years."

I had no qualms about being identified as a Jew, if anything the opposite was true. Maurice and I had decided that as a professional I would wear a Star of David on my boxing shorts. I wanted to show the world who I was, particularly after facing so much antisemitism at school. In wearing the Star of David I was following in the footsteps of an illustrious predecessor, Max Baer.

Born Maximillion Adelbert Baer on 11th February 1909, in Omaha, Nebraska. Max was World Heavyweight Champion from 1934-35. The *Boxing Register*, the International Boxing Hall of Fame Official Record Book, said that Max possessed perhaps, "the most powerful right hand in heavyweight history" and he is rated at number 22 on *The Ring* magazine's list of 100 greatest punchers of all time. In June 1933 Baer started wearing the Star of David on his shorts. That day he defeated Germany's Max Schmeling in front of 60,000 spectators at Yankee Stadium. He said he was doing so to show solidarity with German Jews who were being persecuted by the Nazis.

I had no pretensions of becoming a world champion at that stage of my career but I'd heard all about Max Baer and was proud to emulate him in this way. Many years later I discovered that Baer wasn't Jewish at all. In an article in *Boxing News* legendary trainer Ray Arcel, who guided 20 world champions including Larry Holmes and Roberto Duran, said, "He ain't no Jew, I seen him in the shower." I later discovered there had always been a debate about Baer's Jewishness. His father was a non-practicing Jew and his mother was a Catholic of Scots-Irish descent. Max was raised as a Catholic but he proclaimed himself a Jew as a sign of respect to his father's origins.

Now, just fourteen days after my debut, I entered the ring for my second fight. This time it was my turn to be asked to step in at very short notice. On Monday 3rd June 1985 the St Andrew's Sporting Club hosted the clash for the vacant Scottish Lightweight title between Steve Boyle and Dave Savage, which Boyle won with a technical knock-out in the seventh round. Scheduled on the undercard was a light welterweight contest between Albert Buchanan of Dundee and Nigel Burke of Newport. At lunchtime that day Maurice phoned me to say Buchanan had pulled out and ask if I fancied fighting that night. I gladly volunteered, I'd had a week off to recover after the Conlan fight but I'd been training hard the following week. I knew I was fit and sharp. Plus, I liked the idea of another pay packet.

This would be Burke's third fight. He'd drawn one and lost the other so far so it didn't look as if he would present me with too many problems. And that's how it turned out. After six rounds I was the winner on points again. One report stated, "Jacobs produced all the aggression and worked well to his opponent's midriff."

Body punching was to become my trademark. At the time I had a simple explanation for favouring that tactic. If I aimed for the opponent's face and missed I'd likely hit fresh air. If I aimed for the body and missed the precise target there was a good chance I'd still hit something, like an arm. It's all about connecting. I knew if I could connect I'd deliver pain and that was a good way to stop my opponent.

A month later, on 5th July, the British boxing rankings were published. In the welterweight division I was ranked a lowly 80th out of 105. Lloyd Honeygan was European Champion, Kostas Petrou was the British title holder and Sylvester Mittee held the Commonwealth crown. At that point Maurice wasn't aiming anywhere near those heady heights for me, but he had started plotting the immediate future. He had identified a number of higher-ranked boxers who would, in his opinion, be good match-ups for me. He put black crosses alongside the names of Mike McKenzie who was 78th, Dave Heaver (71st), Courtney Phillips (49th) and Alastair Laurie who was a respectable 26th. In addition, he identified a number of boxers in the light welterweight division. These were Nigel Burke, who was bottom of the pile with a ranking of 55, Tyrell Wilson (47), Albert Buchanan (45) and Billy Cairns who was 21st.

My next fight was on a Jimmy Murray promotion at the Plaza in Glasgow. In the lead-up Murray tried hard to generate interest in the show among the city's Jewish community. He produced a poster which read, "Introducing Gary Jacobs. Boxing promoter James Murray presents a rare chance at the Plaza Ballroom on 12th August. Appearing on the open public show is young Shawlands fighter Gary Jacobs. Gary is the first Glasgow Jewish boxer to be developed to professional standard since Vic Herman, who took Glasgow by storm 37 years ago. The 12th August provides a splendid opportunity for the community to come along and encourage young Jacobs."

Meanwhile, Maurice's masterplan was working like clockwork. My opponent at the Plaza would be none other than Mike McKenzie, who was first on his hit list. The fight, over six two-minute rounds, proved much more difficult than anyone had anticipated. The referee's scorecard gave me just a one-point advantage. Prior to that night McKenzie, from Perth, had a very poor record with just two wins, seven losses and a draw. When he retired less than three years later his career included just seven wins and 21 defeats. He was supposed to be a pushover, but, inexplicably, it was a bit of a close call.

Next up was another on the list, Albert Buchanan. The Dundonian, like McKenzie, was regarded as more cannon fodder. His record coming into the 7th October fight at The County Inn, Cambuslang, was two wins, nine losses and a draw. He was chosen because, on paper, he would prove easy meat for me and boost my confidence, and so it proved. I had him down for a count of eight in the first round and then again in the fifth. This was a much easier points victory. I was just too powerful for Buchanan, who did his best.

I now had four wins out of four and although I was growing in confidence and stature, all my fights to date had resulted in points decisions. Some observers were muttering that my reputation as a hard-hitting amateur was undeserved, but I was unconcerned about the lack of knock-outs on my record.

The professionals were fitter than the amateurs and could withstand greater punishment. I maintained a strict training regime and I knew I was getting stronger and more powerful. It was just a matter of time before it all came together and I landed the knock-out blow. I knew that one night soon someone somewhere would suffer terrible pain at my hands, and unfortunately for Tyrell Wilson, it happened in my next fight. The 27-year-old from Newport was less than a year away from the end of an undistinguished career which would read just 10 wins out of 44 attempts. When he entered the ring against me on the St Andrew's Sporting Club bill at the Albany Hotel, Glasgow on 11th November 1985 he'd already been knocked out eight times while racking up 23 losses. I provided KO number nine courtesy of a right cross to the chin in just over a minute of the fifth round. Maurice could cross a third opponent off his list.

Doncaster-based Dave Heaver was another lamb to the slaughter. Although, for obvious reasons, it wasn't billed that way by promoter Alex Morrison. The programme for the show at the Plaza on 2nd December, just eight days before my 20th birthday, described Ayrshire-born Heaver as "a hard puncher who comes to fight." It was an optimistic assessment considering he arrived in Glasgow having lost 24 fights while winning only seven. At The Plaza, predictably, Heaver was given the heave-ho, but it might have been very different. During the fifth of the scheduled six rounds I lost my balance momentarily and stumbled against referee Len Mullen. I felt a sudden pain in my left ankle and when I got back to the corner Maurice and I knew something was seriously wrong. I couldn't put any weight on my foot and the pain was horrendous. I didn't know it at the time but the ankle was broken. Maurice was unmoved. "There's no way you're chucking this fight," he told me. "Just get out there and hop about for two minutes and make sure he doesn't hit you." It turned out easier than I thought and I even won the last round!

I was six from six now as a pro but Maurice was still ultra-cautious when it came to picking my opponents. His next choice was Taffy Maurice who fought out of Darlington. The Welshman had been knocked out in his last two fights and had been out of action for ten months. It should have been straightforward, but it was not. Taffy pulled out at short notice and in his place along came Courtney Phillips. On the day of the fight, Monday, 10th February 1986, Maurice phoned a promoter who knew a bit about Phillips. He wasn't pleased by what he heard. Phillips, originally from Jamaica, possessed a good amateur record and was described as "a bit of a livewire, a tasty fighter with potential to go far". To add to Maurice's woes Phillips came into the Alex M promotion at the Plaza with a good record of three wins and one defeat. And at first it looked as if Maurice was right to be worried as I was caught by several stiff upper cuts in the second round. As the bell sounded for the third, the vocal home crowd were getting increasingly uneasy. The noise level had dropped considerably, always a bad sign. But suddenly everything clicked into place for me. I had Phillips against the ropes, landing hard punches from all angles to head and body. He seemed to wilt, yet, instead of pressing home my advantage and bringing the contest to a quick end, something made me pause to take stock. It was as if I were basking in my own glory. That short break gave Phillips enough breathing space to survive until the bell. Back in the corner, I was getting a talking to so severe it could be overheard by some of the crowd!

Maurice and I were friendly with a Glasgow jeweller called Alan Morris, who had been to every one of my fights and always insisted on ringside seats. He could clearly hear the words of wisdom directed at me by one of the cornermen, Billy Connelly. Billy's nickname was Basher and he looked as if he was about to bash me. "What the fuck were you doing there?" he roared. "Keep battering him until the ref pulls you off. Don't stand back and admire your fucking handiwork." The message got through. After one minute, 57 seconds of the fifth the fight was over. Phillips required a count of four after taking a barrage of fierce hooks to the head. A few more heavy hits from me forced the referee to stop the fight and save the slippery Phillips from further punishment.

Unlike Connelly, Maurice never shouted in the corner. He kept his cool and got his point across without bawling or swearing. He preferred a wee whisper into my ear ten seconds before the bell would sound to start the next round. The combination worked well that night. John Quinn, legendary boxing correspondent of the *Evening Times* in Glasgow, described the fight as, "the finest display of Gary's career". At the start of my pro career Maurice had pinpointed eight potential opponents he thought I could handle with comfort. It was a testament to his match-making skills that while chalking up seven consecutive victories I had faced six of those on the list. Selkirk's Alastair Laurie would make it the not-so-magnificent seven.

Nine months earlier Laurie had been ranked 54 places above me. Our clash at the Plaza exactly a month after the Phillips fight, on 10th March, would make a mockery of that gap. Laurie's record of nine wins and four defeats was the best among my opponents to date. He'd enjoyed a good amateur career and, while I was favourite to win, many ringside observers quietly fancied the lanky Borderer to upset the applecart, but after eight rounds I was proclaimed the victor by the smallest of margins.

It could have gone either way. In the third round I rocked him with a strong right to the head, but Laurie worked hard to get back into the fight. In the end the result came down to my non-stop aggression throughout, particularly in the final round when my superior strength and fitness allowed me to land a succession of vicious body shots without reply. This bout broke new ground for me. It was the first time the rounds had lasted three minutes. The 24 minutes of non-stop action had been a hard slog, but thanks to my punishing training regime I was still full of energy at the end.

Maurice could have been forgiven had he allowed a smile of self-satisfaction to spread across his face. So far he'd achieved everything he'd set out to do for me. But he was shrewd enough to know it wasn't yet time for back-slapping. That would come later, much later. Phase One of my career path had been negotiated safely. It was time to up the ante. I had proved myself against a bunch of no-hopers. From now on the stakes would be higher and I would face much tougher opposition.

French Toast

ECSTATIC FOLLOWING MY Paris performance, Mickey Duff began making moves to get me that world title fight I had been dreaming of. He wrote to all four boxing commissions asking them to make me the number one contender. As I headed off on a well-earned holiday with my family, the enormity of my achievement began to sink in. Not least because for once I had a fair stack of cash in the bank, thanks to the generosity of French TV who paid £140,000 to stage the first fight and even more for the re-match.

In fact, it seemed as if the French couldn't get enough of me. Mickey was immediately approached about me going back to Paris to make my first title defence. This time my opponent wouldn't be Ludovic Proto, he didn't really fancy his chances of making it third time lucky, instead it was suggested I fight Antoine Fernandez.

Mickey, as shrewd as ever, didn't rush to accept what would be yet another big-money night for me. Fernandez looked as if he might be quite dangerous. He had won the European Welterweight title back in December 1989 and had successfully defended it four months later before losing it to Kirkland Laing. And as recently as 12 months earlier he had lost to current belt holder Patrizo Oliva, so he was no mug. After careful consideration Mickey agreed to the deal. He reckoned Fernandez's career was on the downward slope and so I was all set for an exciting, and lucrative, return to the scene of my greatest triumph.

But as often happens in boxing, things change very quickly and on Wednesday 19th May 1993 I found myself in Sunderland facing Horace Fleary, a former sparring partner. Nobody really knew much about Horace. He was born in the Caribbean, based in Yorkshire but seemed to have some sort of German connection. Along the way he'd beaten one Andreas Schweiger for the vacant German International Super Middleweight crown, whatever that means. He then lost to Nelson Alvez when contesting the Georgian Super Middleweight title. By the time he faced me he'd become the German International Light Middleweight champ. But I was now the European Champion and the chasm in class between us was obvious from the first bell. I picked him off at will and by the end of four rounds he'd retired injured having apparently hurt his knuckle. I reckoned the rest of his body was in considerable agony, too. Unfortunately for me, a clash of heads resulted in a cut on my forehead. That disappointment apart, it was the easiest £10,000 I'd earned in my life.

Meanwhile the French were still at it. They appeared desperate to put up one of their countrymen against me. It was as if they felt their national honour had been tarnished by me and they wanted to restore their Gallic pride. Their latest offering was Daniel Bicchieray and their persistence paid off when Mickey agreed that I would defend my title against him on 22nd September 1993. Although this time the fight would take place in London. By now my thoughts were beginning to focus on a world title fight against Pernell Whitaker. The American was the WBC champ and regarded as the best of all welterweights. Such was my inner confidence, I reckoned I could take him. It was becoming a dangerous obsession, but I just couldn't shake it off.

On the eve of my first, and most important, title defence, I couldn't focus fully on the task at hand. All I could talk about was Whitaker. I told the press, "Whitaker is the best and he is the one I want to face. The WBC is the most prestigious world title and it's the one I want a shot at." Daniel Bicchieray, meanwhile, with a highly-respectable record of 35 wins (16 of them inside the distance), three draws and five defeats, was not totally relegated to the back burner of my brain. I trained hard for the fight and I knew I had to take his awkward high-guarded style seriously, and the hard work paid off when I stopped the Frenchman in the fifth. My tactics against him worked well. I kept behind the jab and forced him to come at me and because of his high stance I found it easy to pick off his body. Eventually he just couldn't handle the punishment and the ref stepped in.

Immediately after what was little more than a brisk workout for me, speculation began in earnest again about a world title fight. It was as if the Bicchieray battle had been merely a support act to the main event, the conversation about my future! The following morning's papers were full of chat about me becoming a dollar millionaire by taking on Pernel Whitaker in America. There were a couple of other scenarios on the go as well. Barney Eastwood was suggesting I could fight WBA welter champ Crisanto Espana, whom he managed at the time. The only snag was he wanted us to put up the million for his boy to come to Glasgow. Mickey showed his contempt for that suggestion by completely ignoring it.

Having lost again, the French were determined to prolong their love-hate affair with me by having another go at me. It wouldn't be long before they would come in with another big-money offer. They were desperate to find one of their countrymen who could beat me. It was becoming a national obsession among boxing fans and, thankfully, the free-spending TV channels over there. Unfortunately for them, they'd run out of top-class home-grown talent. So they conjured up the next best thing – Tek Nkalankete, who wasn't strictly-speaking French.

Born in Zaire, Tek was now based in France and, since they were paying so much for the privilege, the fight was going to take place in Paris. And they were so anxious for a home winner they tried all sorts of underhand techniques to get their way.

Things began to go wrong long before the first bell and

continued well after it, but before all that would come to pass I interrupted my training schedule for a very important family get-together. My second daughter, Jemma, was born on Thursday 20th January 1994 and once again I'm proud to say I was there at Rutherglen Maternity to witness another wonderful day for Linda and me.

Less than two weeks later it was back to business. We were staying in a Parisian hotel and the promoters arranged a taxi to take me to the weigh-in. It took an hour and 15 minutes driving through the city to get there. Yet I was assured the hotel was handy for the venue! Sitting in the back seat I was going nuts because I was worried about being late and getting disqualified. After the weigh-in I told Mickey I wasn't going back in the same cab because I didn't trust the driver. I asked him to phone me another one. The new cab duly arrived and as I got in the driver gave me a funny look. It turned out my hotel was just round the corner. It was an attempt to unsettle me and it worked for a few minutes until I got it out of my system.

What concerned me more was that people in my camp kept reminding me about the first Proto fight, when I was a victim of daylight robbery. They might have been worried but I wasn't. I didn't really fear much from Nkalankete. To me he wasn't exactly high tech. He was a former European Light Welter champion, but that was back in 1987, seven years earlier. He was described as durable and seasoned, but I reckoned that was just a polite reference to his age, 36. I now thought of myself as a genuine world title contender and he hadn't made it to that level. True, he had never been knocked out. "But," I told the media, "there's always a first time" and that scenario almost came to pass in the first round.

I stormed into him with hooks and body punches before a right upper cut forced him to take a count of eight. It should have been all over at that point if the ref had done his job properly and started the count when Tek hit the deck, but he paused for what seemed a very long time before starting. In fact, Dick Currie's ringside report in the *Daily Record* the next day stated, "It took the Italian ref about 20 seconds to start the count when Nkalankete was on the floor." I'm sure that was a bit of an exaggeration but it shows the fight should have been done and dusted inside the first minute. For the rest of that round I continued to slam punches into him and I had him swaying almost defenceless on the ropes. Sadly he was saved by the bell.

I began round two the way I finished the first, landing hooks and upper cuts at will. This established the pattern for the rest of the fight, although he got lucky from time to time when he connected with a few wild swings to my head. His best round came in the fifth when he cut me on the left eyebrow. Meanwhile the ref was doing me no favours, cautioning me for holding and pushing my opponent, who was leaning in to me to avoid punishment. In the eleventh he deducted a point from me for holding, which must have given Nklalankete a glint of hope, even though I was way out in front. However any thoughts he had of making a go of it in the final round were destroyed when I connected with a solid right which left him stunned and wobbling, and although I couldn't finish him off at that point, I knew there was no way back for him.

Of course, on the Continent you can never tell what the officials are going to do. So, even though I had demolished the man from Zaire, there were a few anxious moments before the Italian ref raised my arm in triumph. It was a unanimous decision from him and the two judges. However, that was not the end of the drama.

Three weeks after that fight I got a phone call from Mickey. He said, "You need to fly to Paris tomorrow. You've failed a drugs test." I was stunned. I knew I was clean. Six hours later he phoned back telling me not to worry, the officials had made a mistake. I reckon they confused my sample with Nkalankete's. After the fight I'd hit him so hard and so often that my hands were in agony. Yet he kept going for 12 rounds. I still can't believe he didn't go down and stay down.

My performance that night should have opened the door for a shot at Whitaker. But the European Boxing Union ordered me to defend my title against the number one contender, Italian Allessandro Duran. It was disappointing that another obstacle to a world title fight had been placed in my way, although on the bright side at least the Duran fight would take place in Glasgow. I was looking forward to climbing into the ring in front of a home crowd.

Betting the Farm

ALLESANDRO DURAN AND I had something in common; we both needed to win because both of us had eyes on bigger prizes. The Italian had lost only four times in 38 outings but, significantly, his most recent setback was a defeat at the hands of Eamonn Loughran for the WBO title in Belfast. Afterwards, in what sounded like a similar tale of woe to my experience against Proto first time round, he blamed the judges. Now he saw our fight as a stepping stone for a re-match with Loughran.

As it happens I watched a video of that fight and I reckon Loughran deserved his victory, but only just. I needed to beat the Italian to get a world title shot of my own against Whitaker. His manager, Dan Duva, had promised Mickey they'd open negotiations about a world title clash if I took care of Duran, and I couldn't care less whether he felt he was robbed in Belfast or not. I would do everything to prevent him leaving Glasgow with my European belt.

Not that I felt I needed any help from the judges. I was so confident about winning I promised Duran that if he beat me I'd buy him a farm. He countered by claiming he'd have a big vocal support from his former countrymen in Glasgow and that they would spur him on to victory. But one look at his battered nose told me he'd be lucky to avoid the power of my onslaught once it was unleashed. He had a face that looked as though it was used to taking a good hit and I intended to find out just how many more hits he could endure!

Meanwhile, Mickey was doing his level best to talk up my world title credentials. On the eve of the fight he told the press, "I have a lot of very good fighters but Gary is probably the best. In fact I'd go as far as saying that Gary is one of the finest I've had the pleasure of managing." I'm not sure who that last comment was meant to impress but it was nice of him to say so all the same. He then added, "Of course I am hell-bent on getting Gary a crack at the world title. It's no more than he deserves."

I wasn't paying too much attention to Mickey's public statements at that point. I was fully focused on defeating Duran. The news that Whitaker had retained his world crown four days earlier with a unanimous points verdict over Puerto Rican Sarlos Cardona didn't distract me, even though it was the result I'd been hoping for.

I remember as a young child watching the great Celtic manager Jock Stein being interviewed on TV. His all-conquering nine-in-a-row team was normally competing for several honours at any one time. Yet when asked about the prospects of a forthcoming cup final or glamour Euro tie he would smile genially and tell his interviewer: "We're only taking one game at a time." So instead of mouthing off about what the future might hold I took a leaf out of Jock's book and simply told the press that I was taking it one fight at a time and, ominously for my opponent, I added: "I've got to blank out everything and concentrate on beating Duran." The Italian came from a notable boxing family: His father Carlos was a former world welterweight champion and his brother Maximilio was a former WBA light-heavyweight champ, but they wouldn't be in the ring with him!

The date was 13th April 1994. It was my first fight in Glasgow for 21 months and the Kelvin Hall was packed. It was a great feeling stepping through the ropes in front of my own crowd and the atmosphere was electric. Duran had plenty of fans from the city's sizeable Italian community, some of whom I knew well because I'd dined in their restaurants. In fact, I knew them better than my opponent did, but I also knew not to expect any support from them until after the fight was over, and the fight was over relatively quickly. Certainly by the third round the writing was on the wall and my challenger was on the deck, not once, but twice! The first time a left hook to the face had him down for a count of four. Then, as I scented an easy victory, I moved in for the quick kill. A flurry of fierce body shots proved too much for him and I dropped him for an eight-count. I hoped he would stay down but Duran's corner frantically urged their man to keep going and he just about managed to get up and survive the round.

Few fighters I've faced have been able to withstand so much sustained pressure from me and keep going. But all credit to the man from Ferrara. He made it for another five rounds, although his chances of winning increasingly depended on landing one desperate lucky punch. He didn't and by the eighth it was all over. By then, of course, everybody in the arena, including, I suspect, Duran and his corner, knew the fight was mine. I just needed to do something to convince the judges. I did so by landing a right hook to his head and I knew as soon as it connected that on this occasion he would not be getting up. Apparently he'd said before the fight that he'd never been knocked down before. He was certainly making up for lost time against me!

On the night it appeared to most observers, me included, that I'd carried out a pretty straightforward, but professional, demolition job on a weaker opponent, but later events proved it had been a very impressive performance on my part. Two-and-a-half years after being totally outclassed by me, on 26th October 1996, Duran beat Gary Murray and became the World Boxing Union welterweight champion. Established in January 1995, for about 15 years or so the WBU was a respectable operation, supported by big money from American TV, but it didn't last and now no longer exists. Its champions were not as highly regarded as those ranked by the WBC and WBA, but they were world champions nevertheless and deserved to be treated with respect.

Murray was originally from Renfrew, but his family had

emigrated to South Africa when he was 14 and he was now fighting out of Cape Town. On 26th August 1995 he had beaten American Buck Smith for the WBU crown. He then defended the title successfully three times before losing it to Duran. They had a rematch four months later when the Italian confirmed his superiority. And here's what he had to say in an interview about the Scot he beat, "He hit really hard and played dirty. In our first battle, for the WBU welterweight crown, he broke my face with headbutts and was disqualified during the fifth round. In the rematch, I dominated and got a unanimous decision. Gary Murray was the classic southpaw that nobody ever wants to fight." I wonder how he felt about me then?

All of this was in the future. Back in the present, after the celebrations of my latest triumph had died down I let myself go and indulged in my normal post-fight binge. I didn't drink or smoke and, at this point, hadn't been introduced to the world of illegal narcotics. My only weakness was chocolate. I was, and still am, a chocoholic. So while all my supporters were toasting my success with champagne, I was getting stuck in to the best Cadbury's had to offer. If I'd been a wee bit wiser I would have bought shares in the company and suggested to Mickey he should consider approaching them for a sponsorship deal!

Having stuffed my face to my heart's content my thoughts turned yet again, inevitably, to Mr Whitaker. I was on fire. Within the space of just 71 days I had turned in two outstanding performances. I couldn't wait for my next fight and hoped it would be up against a big name and soon. I was to be disappointed on both counts. It was fully six months before I would step into the ring again and my opponent was someone called Rusty Derouen. Three years earlier the self-styled "Biloxi Bomber" from Mississippi had won the vacant American Boxing Association Welterweight Championship, but he didn't keep it for very long. I wasn't surprised he'd won the title. His opponent, one Larry McCall, had up till then lost 54 of his 66 fights. And after the ABA defeat McCall maintained his unimpressive streak by losing the next four before hanging up his gloves for good with a dismal record of 12 wins and 59 defeats. Yet he forced Derouen to go the distance.

One fight prior to that, Derouen had been stopped by none other than Gary Murray. It might have been a talking point by the time I met Derouen if anybody had heard of Murray at that stage. It would have given the sports writers a coincidence to jump on. But nobody knew Murray, so the papers missed out on a good story. The one story that did get plenty of space was the continued speculation surrounding my world title shot.

Pernell Whitaker had just beaten Buddy McGirt to retain his WBC crown. It was McGirt's second unsuccessful attempt to wrest the title from Sweet Pea and it looked as if he'd had all the chances he was going to get. It meant there was an opening for me to become the number one challenger, with a guaranteed shot at the champion.

First of all I had to take care of business and I had to do it in the unlikely setting of Wolverhampton. The venue was immaterial to me, even though I didn't quite get the logic. Rusty's record was nothing to write home about but, in keeping with my professional approach, I wasn't going to take him for granted. It was the lesson I learned after the Mickey Hughes debacle, now I was going to teach Rusty a thing or two.

Right from the first bell it was clear he was struggling against my southpaw style and in the first four rounds he hardly landed a punch. Meanwhile I was picking him off with body and head shots. As the fight progressed it was clear Rusty was living up to his name. He just didn't have a clue where my next punch was coming from. In the fifth I upped the pace and began hitting him with powerful body punches, my trademark. Near the end of the round he was so winded he went down on one knee and took an eight count, but the bell came before I could finish him off. At the start of the sixth I chased him into a corner and laid into him with both fists almost at will. After 51 seconds the ref had seen enough and ended the contest. Considering the punishment he'd taken Derouen had lasted quite well, but everyone agreed it was another world-class display by me and my American opponent, for all his bravery, never stood a chance.

Mickey reckoned it was the best performance he'd seen from me and promised he'd start negotiating the next day with Whitaker's management over a world title fight. It was now only a matter of time before I would be ranked second in the world and the champ would have to fight me, whether he liked it or not. In fact, once the rankings were published to confirm my status none of the reigning title-holders - Whitaker, Ike Quartey or Felix Trinidad - could justify ignoring me. But given the choice I wanted Whitaker. He was regarded as the best of the three and that's how I wanted to be known. At that point in my career I genuinely believed I was good enough.

Sadly, it looked like there was no way the fight would take place in Glasgow. There just didn't seem to be enough of an appetite in Scotland for staging a world title fight. The local TV bosses didn't appear too bothered about the prospect, and if we managed to tempt Sweet Pea to the UK, it was almost certain that the venue would be London's Royal Albert Hall. Mickey reckoned the age-old religious bias in Glasgow was to blame. He would mutter, "The trouble with Gary is he's not green, he's not blue, he's a fucking Jew." I knew Mickey wasn't being antisemitic because he himself was Jewish and, of course, I knew from bitter personal experience that there was a strong chance he was right.

The late, great Alex Cameron, at that time the country's most respected sports writer, had this to say in *The Daily Record* soon after the Derouen triumph: "Scots should be deeply ashamed of the treatment given to Gary Jacobs. He's first in line for a world contest after a midweek win - in downtown Wolverhampton - and is already European Champion. His title isn't one of the ready-made phonies which come off the shelf at the drop of a hat. Yet Scots don't rally to Jacobs as they did to Ken Buchanan, Jim Watt, Walter McGowan or Peter Keenan. I can't think why, because he's a decent bloke and a very good boxer. He's an honest-to-goodness pro-puncher who deserves to meet American world title holder Pernell Whitaker. Because of the lukewarm backing by his ain folk, Jacobs will almost certainly have to fight him in London. SHAME ON US!"

The funny thing was, I didn't give a damn where I fought Whitaker. I would gladly have taken him on in his own back garden if I had to. Mickey reckoned I needed two, maybe three, warm-up fights before I was ready for Whitaker and the first of these came just over a month after I had sent Derouen on the road to ruin.

My next opponent was Argentinian veteran Marcelo Domingo Di Croce. The 31-year-old had spent most of his career fighting in his native country and at various times had held the South American, Argentinian and Mundo Hispano Welterweight titles. By the time we met at the London Arena I had relinquished my European title. There was no point hanging on to it because I was now the WBC's number one contender. If I'd kept the Euro crown I would have been required to defend it and right now I had more important things on my mind. Every fight, every training session, was designed to prepare me for a world title showdown against Whitaker. Nothing else mattered.

De Croce's record looked pretty impressive with 55 wins, nine losses and five draws, so he couldn't be underestimated, even if I was expected to win conclusively. I hoped he would give me a good, solid work-out over the distance. Mickey made it clear he wanted a good show from me. His plan was for my next fight to take place in the USA on the supporting bill when Whitaker made his next voluntary defence. Up till now I was always able to focus my attention on my immediate opponent, but not this time. There was so much talk of a world title clash it was beginning to get to me.

And perhaps the prospect of what lay ahead for once dominated my thoughts because after ten rounds I emerged victorious but the performance wasn't up to scratch. True, I had won seven of the ten rounds and I had put him down three times, but it's a measure of how far I had progressed recently that most observers, myself included, reckoned I had an off night. Di Croce proved to be a slippery customer. He held on to me and prevented me from unleashing too many big shots. He actually went down eight times during the fight. Five of those were as a result of his own awkwardness. He either tumbled or slipped, although there were times, when I was turning the screw, when he seemed to go down on one knee a bit too easily. My plan had been to dominate proceedings while avoiding any nasty shocks (like a lucky knock-out punch or a cut) which might put the Whitaker clash at risk. I succeeded but it was a workmanlike rather than spectacular effort.

A few years earlier the commentators might have been waxing lyrical about such an easy victory, but against De Croce it was up to Mickey to put a brave face on things by saying, "It's very hard if you want to waltz and the other guy wants to tango." It was more of a tangle than a tango but it took me two steps nearer Whitaker.

Despite that disappointment, Mickey was true to his word and within four months I came face-to-face with the champ. Unfortunately for me I wasn't fighting him. We met in the opulent surroundings of the Caesar's Complex, Atlantic City. Whitaker was top of the bill and I was on the undercard. That night he would step up a weight division and take on and beat Julio Cesar Vasquez, holder of the WBA light middleweight crown. It was an interesting match-up. Vasquez was five inches taller and his reach was 10 inches longer. Apparently that was the kind of challenge Pernell liked. It was certainly a controversial fight. Whitaker needed a standing count of eight in the fourth round but recovered to produce a great display. His opponent, meanwhile, had points deducted twice for hitting behind the head. Many in the crowd felt the ref was rather harsh on Vasquez.

In the end everyone thought Sweet Pea was worth the victory and his sixth world title, but the final points margin was too wide. It was clearly closer than the officials judged it to be and the result was greeted with booing, but I didn't see the fight because by that stage I was in hospital getting emergency treatment!

Earlier in the night I had to endure a torrid time against Jose Miguel Fernandez. In the fourth round I had connected with a vicious right uppercut. The impact caused a three-inch gash on my fist which left me in agony every time I hit him. It was like being stabbed by a knife in my hand. I had to keep going through the pain barrier. I knew if I gave in to the injury I would lose my number one contender spot. And that just wasn't going to happen. I had come too far and endured too much to give up now. Initially I had planned to KO the New Yorker. I was quite confident of being able to do so and I knew it would look good on American TV. The injury made that less likely but I still tried. Nobody else had a clue about what was going on inside my glove and there was no way I was going to let anyone know I was in trouble.

In the end I ground out a hard-fought points victory against a far from illustrious opponent, winning every round. Back in the dressing room the full extent of my suffering was laid bare for all to see when I removed my gloves to reveal blood-soaked bandages. Mickey Duff reckoned he'd never seen a cut like it in his life. I was taken to hospital and had to wait with a bunch of drunks and junkies for treatment in accident and emergency before getting seven stitches. It would be six weeks before the wound would heal completely.

On the plus side, what was seen by Whitaker's camp as a lacklustre display by me would probably lead them to underrate me. That afternoon, before all the drama unfolded in the ring, the champ and I had enjoyed a friendly wee chat. Typically, the man opposite me did most of the talking. He said, "There's been talk of me taking on the WBA world welterweight champion Ike Quartey in my next fight - but I want Jacobs. He's my mandatory defence and I won't deprive an up-and-coming challenger of that chance. Scotland has a boxer to be proud of. Gary deserves his chance, but I am a master of this sport and it will be a good lesson for him."

I muttered something about taking care of Fernandez before thinking of a world title shot. It sounded cool but inside I was bursting with excitement at the prospect of finally fighting the world champion.

I was almost, but not quite, speechless!

Nervous but Determined

Before my crack at the world title could take place there were all sorts of issues to finalise. Mickey Duff was desperate to bring my showdown with Pernell Whitaker to Glasgow and reckoned he needed a £1 million package to succeed and made his public plea for support. "If we could get Glasgow District Council to give us the large Kelvin Hall arena, if we can get sponsorship of £100,000, if we can get TV backing, and if the fans rally round we can get it off the ground. I know there are many drawbacks but we have faced them before in the great days when Jim Watt was world lightweight champion. Those days were of immense mutual benefit for Jim and the city when everyone played their part - and I honestly believe Gary can do the same.

"Realistically, it is a long shot but, as you know, I just love a challenge and I am prepared to do everything in my power to get this fight for Gary in Glasgow. You can never tell how things bounce in this business. They may just bite if we make them the right offer. However, if Gary was to get £200,000 instead of say, £50,000 here, then we would go to America. That certainly holds no fears for Gary and none for me. It would complete a great hat-trick for us, having taken John H Stracey to Mexico City to beat Jose Napoles in 1975 and Lloyd Honeyghan to Atlantic City to beat Don Curry in 1986. Neither were given any chance of victory but brought home world titles. There is no reason why Gary can't do likewise."

While I would have loved Mickey to succeed and bring the fight to Glasgow, I had a strong feeling it was wishful thinking on his part. It didn't bother me though. I was just happy to get my big chance and I didn't care where it happened. In the end Mickey had to accept the inevitable and the contest was set for Saturday 26th August 1995 at the Convention Hall, Atlantic City.

I was under no illusions about the size of the task ahead of me. As far as I was concerned I had to knock the champ out to win. I reckoned the man dubbed 'the best pound-for-pound boxer in the world today' would prevail if the fight went the distance. Not because I was inferior to him in any way, I just felt I wouldn't be allowed to win on his home turf. I also believed I had the stronger punch and that my power would wear him down.

My preparations included going back to the Catskills for a month before the fight, then moving to Atlantic City with just three days to go. Up till now I had never been away from my wife, Linda, and my daughters, Olivia and Jenna, for more than a week, so I was full of mixed emotions as I flew out of Glasgow for my date with destiny. On the one hand, we had a close-knit family and being a boxer meant I didn't need to be at work all day. I could be at home, watching my darling daughters grow up and, believe me, having the opportunity to spend so much time with my children was the greatest bonus I could think of. On the other hand I had a job to do. I had to support my loved ones and provide for them.

Under normal circumstances I didn't like my family being too close to me when I was preparing for a fight. They provided just too many distractions. And, as this was the fight of my life, I couldn't afford even the tiniest interruption during my preparations. So we agreed that Linda would fly to the States just two days before I entered the ring. She wouldn't watch me in person, though. She hated getting a close-up view of me taking hard knocks and preferred to see the action from the safety of her hotel room. On this occasion that decision almost landed her in jail, but there was no hint of any trouble as I headed out for what I knew would be my toughest challenge yet.

As we crossed the Atlantic at 35,000 feet I was in a reflective mood and couldn't help analysing my position. The Yanks had virtually written me off, but they didn't know me very well. They didn't realise just how much winning the world title would mean to me. It was said the bookies in Atlantic City were offering 20/1 against me. I knew that was ludicrously generous and intended to stick a few quid on myself. I was really up for a right old scrap and I took inspiration from the last British welterweight who won in America. Nine years earlier Lloyd Honeyghan was given no chance by the so-called experts when he went to Atlantic City to face Don Curry, who at that time held the WBC, WBA and IBF titles. Like my opponent, Curry was regarded as the best pound-for-pound boxer in the world. Yet he was forced to retire after just six rounds against a highly-motivated Honeyghan.

I knew I could have fought for another world title against a lesser opponent, Eamonn Loughran for example, but deep down I wanted Whitaker's crown because he was the best and by beating him I would become the best. It wasn't about money, either, although this was certainly the most lucrative fight on offer. It was about recognition. I knew if I won this world title respect for me would be total and I really wanted to be up there with the greats. There were signs, too, that my opponent's preparations weren't quite going to plan. Whitaker had just sacked his lifelong trainer, George Benton, and I reckoned it showed he was feeling the heat a bit. It would be akin to me dumping Maurice Lewis. It was something that would just never occur to me under any circumstances.

As we approached New York City I thought back to the day I first met Maurice. I'd travelled a long and winding road since then. He'd been with me every step of the way and I took comfort from the fact he was still there, sitting next to me. I also took comfort when I arrived at my training camp at the luxurious Concord Resort in The Catskill Mountains. I'd been there seven years earlier in August 1989 during the build-up to my fight with Buddy McGirt. If anything, it had become even more luxurious since then and, let me tell you, that was no mean feat. I couldn't believe so much time had passed since my last visit. I'd had 19 fights since then and had won every title I'd gone for. Yet, strangely, I rarely thought of the triumphs. My memories kept returning to the events on the night of the 17th October 1990. It wouldn't be inaccurate to say I was still haunted by them.

I was up against Englishman Mickey Hughes in a fight I was expected to win easily. Mickey had turned pro a few months after I did in 1985 and retired with an undistinguished record in 1993. The official reports state he knocked me out in the eighth round of a scheduled ten-rounder and that, "Hughes was behind on points". This was a monumental understatement. In reality, I doubt if Mickey had landed a single glove on me throughout the first seven rounds. I was probably as fit as I'd ever been and had enjoyed the luxury of two great sessions with legendary trainer Teddy Atlas in the build-up. Mickey never stood a chance.

Yet from nowhere he produced a punch that not only floored me to end the fight, it left me dazed and confused in a hospital ward for several hours afterwards. It was certainly the hardest hit I had ever taken. And yet I took a great deal of solace from that experience, which was painful in more ways than one.

I was back in action within five months and then went on an amazing unbeaten run. On 16th October 1992, exactly two years later, I was fighting Ludovic Proto for the European title. In that space of time I had learned two very important lessons from the Hughes defeat and its aftermath. The first was that even a boxer who is being totally outclassed can dig in and pull off a shock victory. It made me realise that so long as I was still standing I could beat my opponent, regardless of how good he might be. That self-belief would be crucial when I took on Whitaker. The other lesson I learned is that I could take a beating and fight back!

And so, for the next three weeks, under Maurice's watchful eye, I trained, ran and ate carefully, which meant no chocolates or other sweet temptations. That was easier said than done because the food at The Concord was amazing and there was so much of it. After the first few days I ignored the sumptuous spreads that were, seemingly, available 24/7 and knuckled down to a monastic existence.

The hotel was situated around 2,000 feet above sea level and it took a while to get used to the altitude. But I knew when I headed to Atlantic City, back at sea level, my lungs would find it a lot easier and that could only be a good thing once I stepped into the ring. The set-up was first class. The boxing ring was championship standard and I had all the training kit I could dream of. And there was an added bonus. I agreed to make one of my training sessions each day an "open" event. This meant that the other hotel guests could come and watch.

So every day at 12.30 I would perform in front of dozens of people, mostly Americans, who were definitely on my side. Their constant support and encouragement certainly gave me extra confidence. In return I tried to put on a bit of a show for them — mainly at the expense of some of my sparring partners. One had to retire after a ferocious hook burst his ear drum, another had the misfortune to hit me with a low blow. I lost my rag just a wee bit and set about him with all my power, leaving him a bit of a wreck on the ropes.

Suddenly, it was a week before the fight and everybody around me was getting excited. The Scottish press had arrived in force and there were interviews to be done almost every hour, it seemed. After three weeks in the training camp I felt tense but confident as I discussed the monumental task ahead of me.

I was even fond of repeating a joke I'd heard:
Me - Knock, knock.
Reporter - Who's there?
Me – Pernell.

Reporter - Pernell who?

Me - That's boxing.

I wasn't deliberately demeaning my opponent, it was just my way of dealing with the pressure. I was also upbeat about my chances. I told Phil McEntee of the *Sunday Express*: "I'm going to win the title and cash in on ten years of hard work. Whitaker has taken part in 16 world title fights and won four at different weights so he has a bit of a record. I have to respect what he has achieved but I will not show him any undue respect in the ring. He is a small man, older than me at 31, a southpaw who hates fighting southpaws like me and not popular with the American people. This is going to be my night."

Mickey Duff told other pressmen, "You never know with fighters. Sometimes, once they reach a certain age, they suddenly wake up in the morning and find out that they're an old man. I'm not saying that will happen with Whitaker but it might."

Meanwhile, the *Scottish Sun* had arranged for me to write a big fight diary. Obviously I didn't do the writing, but I supplied the material to reporter Ewing Grahame. Here's a flavour of my life at Concord, as reported in the diary's first entry:

"As if I needed an extra incentive to beat Whitaker, I can exclusively reveal that my wife Linda is expecting our third child on 1st February. I already have two daughters, Jenna and Olivia, so I must be a glutton for punishment! However, the title itself is all the motivation I really need to work hard. By the time I'll have finished I'll have sparred over 100 rounds. I get up at 6am to do my road work. Six miles before breakfast sets me up for the day. My gym work - sparring, skipping, bodywork and the speed bag - is usually over by 2pm. That leaves the rest of the day free for swimming, tennis and golf. Yesterday I played nine holes at one of the golf courses here. It's so spectacular it makes Gleneagles look shabby.

"I've usually worked up an appetite after that but last night I excelled even myself. I had melon for starters, a roast chicken, THREE steaks then dessert. I could never eat like that at home!" So far so good I thought. But Mickey was furious.

Five days before the fight the WBC announced the appointment of New Yorker Ron Lipton as referee. Mickey had expected a referee from a neutral country and decided to launch a formal protest saying, "It's just not fair to appoint an American when one of the boxers is from this country." The promoters tried to diffuse the row by stating that Lipton was highly-experienced and that the judges will come from three neutral countries - Japan, Hawaii and Australia. Most observers reckoned the WBC were showing favouritism towards Whitaker. As usual I left controversies like that to my manager, preferring to focus on my own preparations. Mickey liked to moan about everything, while I knew if I knocked out the champ it wouldn't matter if the referee was his brother!

The promoters did, however, manage to disrupt my schedule by insisting that I leave my training camp a day earlier than planned and travel to Atlantic City for a joint press conference with Whitaker. When I got there Whitaker was holding court and sparring in front of the TV cameras. There was no press conference and I left soon after arriving. It had been a total waste of my time, time I could have devoted to training.

I wasn't annoyed, though. I'd been involved in some dirty tricks in the past and by comparison this was minor. But it just showed you that the promoters and the WBC wanted the title to stay with Whitaker and would do anything they could to ensure that happened. I wasn't bothered because, with so much at stake, I expected something like this to happen.

This was the first sign that the fight was nearly upon us, that the waiting and training was nearly over. The second sign was when Whitaker started shooting from the lip. Maybe ticket sales were slow or maybe he was just a big mouth, but suddenly there he was, telling everyone precisely what he was going to do to me when we finally met. Sweet Pea boasted,

"I'm going out to have some fun with Gary - it's not personal, it's just business, poor guy. He's simply not in my class and I'm going make it look easy and simple against him. I love going the whole 12 rounds but I'll put pressure on all the time and try to get out of there as quickly as I can. This is Gary's big opportunity - it's his first title fight but it's my 17th and I'm definitely going to win. I'll put on a great performance.

"I've done all my homework and the customer will see me put on a show. This is the best shape I've been in since September 1993. I can't put my finger on it but I feel just great. It doesn't make any difference what he does. If he comes to pressure it will make it a good fight. I'm going in there to do a job, do a number on him. If he cooperates he could go in the first round. I don't care if he has eight hands. If he can fight then he's going to have to show it. If he can't fight then I'm sorry.

"I have been able to reach back and rediscover some of my lost youth. Some of the old moves have been dusted down and the fans are in for a real treat. They are going to be shaking their heads in amazement at some of the things I will be doing. I'm going to do it all. I'm going to really dazzle. He might have been British, European and Commonwealth Champion, but you have to fight here to prove yourself. This is America."

I didn't want to get drawn into a war of words. It just wasn't me. However, with so many Scottish sportswriters around it was impossible to decline to comment. So I responded in my usual, measured way. "Maybe that kind of talk gets to some other fighters but it doesn't bother me at all. If he thinks going in against me is going to be fun then he'll have another thing coming."

I was cool on the outside, but inside there was a lot going through my mind. The enormity of the situation had finally sunk in. Three months of hard training in Glasgow followed by a month-long training camp in the USA as preparation to take on the best fighter on earth in front a worldwide TV audience of millions. I was feeling the pressure. Despite that the thought of losing never entered my mind. I knew I was good and that I fully deserved this opportunity. I had been dreaming of this moment for many years.

I was so confident, I even told one reporter that I'd make my first defence against Buddy McGirt. Apparently, the American press were using that contest to highlight my weaknesses. It didn't bother me. Nothing did at that point. After taking out Whitaker I would show the Yanks that the McGirt result was down to my inexperience and nothing else. I was planning to fight every round as if it were my last. I knew I wasn't the world's most stylish boxer but I was at my peak mentally and physically. I was going to be the world champion - and nobody would stand in my way. And at least one highly-regarded boxing commentator agreed with me. This was Ewing Grahame's pre-fight prediction in *The Sun*:

> *Gary Jacobs will pull off one of the most astonishing upsets in boxing history by stopping ring legend Pernell Whitaker to take the WBC welterweight crown. Like most people I feared Whitaker would have too much class and big fight experience for the Scot. But after seeing the Glaswegian in action in the gym, I'm convinced he has an even chance of bashing the bookies as well as cocky champ Whitaker.*
>
> *Gary's fitness, strength and determination are at an all-time high. He's also punching harder than ever before - as his sparring partners would readily testify. That power punching could hold the key to the outcome. Gary's punishing body shots - if he's allowed to work inside by Yank referee Ron Lipton - could be the crucial element of the bout.*
>
> *Whitaker has been a great champion at four different levels and it's not that Gary is taking him lightly when he says that he will stop him. However, all eras must come to an end and it could be that Whitaker - not the greatest puncher in the world - will find he's taken one tough contest too many when he faces the Scot.*

I was desperate to prove him right

Tom Fitzsimmons was, and still is, a good pal. He owned a very successful business called Deutsche Tune Body Shop, which was Europe's largest Porsche repair centre. He was also one of my sponsors and gave me a nice little Porsche to run around with. He and two other pals — Stevie Fraser and Michael Antoniou — who had been to many of my fights, were with me now in Atlantic City. We'd agreed they would march with me into the ring, kitted out in kilts and carrying Scotland flags. The three of them appeared in the dressing room about 45 minutes before the fight, but I was too preoccupied with my own thoughts to engage with them, other than to exchange brief greetings.

Afterwards, when it was all over, Tom told me they'd had to walk past Whitaker's changing room to get to mine and it was going like a fair. The door was open and they could see it was stowed out with people, all laughing and joking and having a good time. There were plenty of girls there, music was blaring and Sweet Pea was mixing freely with his entourage. He looked relaxed and the place had a party feel about it. My dressing room was more like a morgue by comparison. Tom even went as far as saying there was a bad atmosphere in the room. He couldn't put his finger on it, but to him something wasn't right. It was too tense, there was none of the usual pre-fight banter. Tom and the others were so uncomfortable they went outside and sat in the hallway for a while.

Yet, as I prepared for the fight of my life, I was unaware of all that nor did I care about it. It was quiet in my changing room which, considering the glamorous venue, was a bit of a dump. It reminded me of the days I played football with Maccabi when we'd get stripped in concrete huts with bare walls, no heating and a couple of rickety wooden benches. Like them this one was small, cold and basic. While no expense was spared for the rest of the building, it was as if this changing room had been added as an after-thought. It was more like a cubby-hole where cleaners stored their material. Perhaps that's what it had once been?

It was busy: Tom, Stevie and Michael popped in to wish me good luck and hung around waiting for me in silence. Maurice was there, as were Mickey Duff and cut man Dennie Mancini. WBC officials checked the bandaging round my hands and gave me the all-clear. Nobody was doing much talking. Everything had already been said. From now on only deeds would count.

In my head there was one thought I repeated over and over again — I was here to win the world title, not just fight for it. I was so focussed on victory I took no notice of what was going on around me as I followed the piper, who was blasting out 'Scotland the Brave', and my three amigos through the crowd before climbing into the ring. The introductions and instructions passed in a blur. I couldn't wait to get started. I wanted to feel my glove connect with my opponent's flesh. The bell sounded and I moved cautiously towards the centre of the ring.

The film of the fight is now on YouTube and you can judge for yourself how I got on.

But here, for the first time, is my personal Big-Fight round-by-round verdict, with Sweet Pea's score first. The American scoring system meant that the winner of each round would get 10 points and the loser nine. However, if one fighter was knocked down the judges could deduct one or more points from his score on that round.

ROUND ONE—In my view this was very close, but only one of the judges made it a draw. The other two gave it to Whitaker. The commentators said I was awkwardly and cleverly effective. My score:10-10.

ROUND TWO—Followed a similar pattern to the first but Whitaker was more accurate and landed better punches.

Despite the fact I had landed a greater percentage of punches in each of the first two rounds I agree with the three judges who gave him the round, but only just. My score: 20-19.

My tactics were simple—to get in close and hurt him with my trademark body shots and so far I had succeeded rather well. I got in very close almost at will but I knew I hadn't really landed a powerful hit up to that point.

ROUND THREE—The ref's decisions started to go against me. Immediately after I landed a clean right hook to the champ's head I was warned about using my head. Despite that I knew I'd won the round comfortably. Two of the judges agreed with me, while one scored it a draw. My score: 29-29.

So a quarter of the fight had gone and there was nothing between me and the world's greatest boxer. I was feeling good at this point.

ROUND FOUR—Whitaker, urged by his worried corner, changed tactics slightly and began to take me on at my own game by working harder inside. Until now he relied more on trying to pick me off with his jab. He also caught me with a couple of good long shots, including a clear hit right on the centre of my nose. It was his round, just. My score: 39-38. Curiously, the commentators had it all square at this point. Meanwhile, one of the judges agreed with me while the other two had Whitaker two rounds in front.

ROUND FIVE—Early on I got a warning for using my elbows. To be fair to the ref he called it right. Whitaker also got a warning, for holding. We traded a lot of blows but overall he probably landed more of the better punches so I give him the round. My score: 49-47.

ROUND SIX—Whitaker again scored plenty of clean hits but, although they might have looked good, none of them hurt me. The style and tempo of the fight hadn't altered since the first bell. I wanted to get in close and land body shots, while he tried to pick me off with his fast jab from afar. I knew I would take a bit of punishment in order to achieve my goal, but since he really couldn't hurt me it was a risk worth taking. Whitaker was also starting to use his head and constantly tried to butt me in the clinches. At one point I gestured to the ref about it but he completely ignored me. Having said all that I think he shaded the round due to the quality of his punches. My score: 59-56.

At the halfway stage the fight was going pretty much as I expected it to. I'd always said I would need a knock-out to win and that opinion hadn't changed. Technically he was superior to me but I had the bigger punch. The judges' view at that stage was, by and large, similar to mine. Their scoring was 59-56, 59-55 and 60-56. As we entered the second half I expected the champ to tire a little and hoped that would allow me a few good opportunities to land a big blow. I was still as fit and as strong as I had been at the start.

ROUND SEVEN—His best so far. I just couldn't get close to him and he seemed to pick me off at will. I was the one who was beginning to tire. I'd have to stop the rot in the next round otherwise things would go from bad to worse. My score: 69-65. At ringside the commentators had it 68-65.

ROUND EIGHT—This was much better than the previous one for me but I still wasn't connecting properly. Neither was he, though, and we spent most of the time grappling. There was nothing in it. My score: 78-75.

ROUND NINE—Scrappy, but I had him against the ropes in the corner. Although I didn't manage to land any heavy clear-cut punches, I showed a great deal of aggression and for that reason I would award that round to me. My score: 87-85.

ROUND TEN—Another good one for me. I caught Whitaker with a couple of good powerful shots and dominated for most of the three minutes. However, he came back at me near the end and probably did enough to earn a draw. My score: 97-95. Coincidentally, the commentators scored it exactly the same. The judges, meanwhile, had departed planet earth and were now living in cloud cuckoo land. One scored it 99-92, another had it 98-92, while the third was 99-93.

ROUND ELEVEN—I finally get a knockdown. Early in the round I connected with a right to his body. It wasn't a great punch but in trying to evade it Whitaker lost his balance and went down. The ref certainly saw it as a knockdown and gave him a count of eight before hostilities were resumed. Now many people, including the commentators who analysed it in slow motion, reckoned it wasn't a proper knockdown, but it doesn't really matter. The ref gave it and the judges had to score it accordingly, which meant Whitaker lost two points—one for the knockdown and one for losing the round. Only one judge scored it according to the book. Incredibly, one judge, American Tomotsu Tomihara, awarded the round to Whitaker! Obviously I wasn't aware of what was happening with the scorecards. I just knew I'd won the round. My score: 105-105.

And so, going into the final round with the world's greatest pound for pound boxer it was pretty close. He couldn't hurt me and I still believed I could damage him. As the bell sounded I knew it was all or nothing now.

ROUND TWELVE—Unfortunately, it all went wrong in those final three minutes. I was struggling. I had very little energy left. I had basically punched and run myself into the ground. I needed a miracle. Instead I got a ref who did my opponent a huge favour. Throughout the fight we'd both been holding. It had been a feature of the contest for 11 rounds. I don't think there is any evidence which would suggest I was guiltier than Whitaker. Yet, in that last round, the ref decided to deduct a point from me because I was holding. Only he can explain why he did it. Sadly, I took it really badly and lost heart from that point on. Near the end of the round Whitaker hit me solidly with a good combination and knocked me down. I was up pretty sharply but there was no question I was stunned. A few seconds later he connected again and I was down again. This time I got up even quicker, but it didn't matter. The bell went and the fight was over.

The score in that final round was 10-6 to Whitaker. The most I could get was nine points but I lost three—one each for the warning and the two knockdowns. So my final tally reads: 115-111 in Whitaker's favour. The judges (Gus Mercurio from Australia, Tomihara from Hawaii and Takeaki Kanaya from Japan) had it 118-109, 118-107 and 117-109 respectively. In round terms it meant that Mercurio decided Whitaker had won 10 rounds, lost one and drawn one, while Tomihara and Kanaya made it 10-2 in his favour. In the final analysis these figures are pretty meaningless. I lost fair and square to a better fighter. He was fitter, faster, stronger and a superb technician. Although there wasn't a huge gap between us, I felt on reflection that the divide was too large for me to bridge at this stage of my career.

I just didn't have the ammunition to compete with someone of Whitaker's quality and experience, who had won world titles at four different weights. I'd done my best and it just wasn't good enough on the night. Perhaps if the fight had been in Glasgow home advantage may have worked in my favour. I wasn't despondent about my performance, the opposite in fact. I actually did pretty well. Well enough to scare Whitaker's people from offering a rematch.

It was my first world title bid and I learned a lot from it, perhaps more than from all my other fights combined. One major difference this time was the amount of sustained pressure I was put under by my opponent. I had never experienced anything like that before, it was relentless.

I was looking forward to making use of that knowledge in my next world championship bid. As far as I was concerned there were three other world crowns and I desperately wanted one of them. Whitaker was the best and I nearly succeeded. The others may not be as difficult.

Some people, including those close to me, reckoned I was putting on a brave face, and to a certain extent that was true. That's because I really believed I could beat Whitaker and it came as a shock to me when I didn't. It was a major setback, no question about it. Winning would have meant financial security for my family and would have put me up there with other boxing legends. But losing wasn't the end of the world. I'd always been super confident, maybe even arrogant. That confidence had been badly dented but I knew I would bounce back.

Whitaker was a generous winner, saying, "I pay full tribute to Gary Jacobs. He was well prepared, fought a great fight and fully deserves to retain his position as No. 1 contender. He certainly didn't come to lie down. For four or five rounds I didn't know what in the world he was doing and it took me a while to figure him out." A couple of members of his management team came into my changing room afterwards and congratulated me on putting up such a good show. They knew I'd given their man a close fight. To the Yanks I'd been an unknown no-hoper but I'd surprised a lot of people and now my credibility at this level was established. HBO announcer

Larry Merchant was impressed by what he saw from me. He said: "The old-timers like myself, who have covered boxing for a long time over here see Whitaker as a one-off. There has not been anyone like him in boxing for 50 years and it was no disgrace to lose to such a brilliant champion."

Daniel Herbert was at ringside for *Boxing News* and he was full of praise for my performance. He wrote: "He didn't win the fight but he won something just as precious – respect, for himself and the sport." Daniel was comparing my fight to the Mike Tyson-Peter McNeeley fiasco which had shocked boxing exactly seven days earlier. Tyson had been due to face the Undisputed Heavyweight Champion Evander Holyfield on 8th November 1991. However, before that could take place he was convicted of raping 18-year-old Desiree Washington and sent to jail for six years. Upon his release, after serving three years, on 25th March 1995, his first comeback fight would be against the little-known Peter McNeeley on 19th August 1995. It lasted only 89 seconds with an easy Tyson victory. McNeeley's manager jumped into the ring to save his man after he was floored twice, the first time with just 10 seconds on the clock. Despite that, it was one of boxing's biggest financial successes with a global audience paying almost $100 million for the privilege of witnessing the one-sided debacle. The outcome shouldn't have been much of a surprise. McNeeley arrived at the MGM Grand in Las Vegas with what looked like a highly-respectable record on paper. He won 24 fights before losing for the first time, then followed that up with another 12 victories on the trot. But the biggest night of his career so far had been at the Westin Hotel, Boston where he lost in an attempt to win the vacant New England Heavyweight Title. So there was no real surprise when the wide gap in class became evident so early on after the first bell.

Afficionados like Daniel Herbert had been far from impressed with Tyson's opponent, which is one reason he wrote so enthusiastically about my performance: "Scotland's

Gary Jacobs helped restore some credibility to boxing and establish himself on the world stage in the process with a valiant challenge. Yes, Whitaker won a unanimous 12-round decision to retain his title but the sell-out crowd saw a real fight for their money – and that was in large part due to the commitment of the Glasgow southpaw. For 11 rounds he fought with such tenacity that he made Whitaker – who disputes the title of best fighter in the world with Roy Jones – look distinctly ordinary, and it was only a disastrous last round which threatened to ruin what had been otherwise an exemplary display by the challenger. Jacobs had a point deducted for holding by unimpressive New Jersey referee Ron Lipton and was then floored twice, being saved by the final bell. That round gave the scores a lopsided feel, with Tomatosu Tomihara of Hawaii the widest at 118-107.

"The Jacobs camp were also unhappy with the scoring of the 11th round in which the Scot is credited with having knocked the normally slippery champion down. Although TV replays suggested, and both boxers later accepted, that the champion had gone down as a result of a slip, referee Lipton ruled it a knock-down and tolled the mandatory eight count. Under WBC rules that should have resulted in a point being deducted from Whitaker's score for the round, regardless of whether he won, lost or shared it. Yet while judge Kanaya gave it to Gary 10-8 and Mercurio awarded it to the Scot by 10-9, Tomihara somehow managed to score it 10-9 to Whitaker."

Of course, after it was all over there was controversy and recrimination. These post- and pre-fight wars of words had become a feature of my career and this was no different. Mickey Duff, while conceding the better fighter won, was furious. He was particularly scathing about the conduct of Larry Hazard, boxing controller of the state of New Jersey and intended to submit an official complaint, even though he knew it would probably be ignored. "His behaviour and language at the weigh-in was appalling. During one of the round breaks he was seen telling the referee how to control the fight — that's something I've never seen before — and when Gary had been knocked down for the second time, he was at the referee to call it a technical knockout, but that was nonsense." Then Mickey had a go at the judges, "Sometimes you have to take a stand on a point of principle and teach these people a lesson. If one of these judges had been in charge of the Kray trial, the twins would have got probation."

As Mickey held court, I got to grips with defeat in the changing room, completely unaware of the drama involving my wife and mother taking place just outside the door. They'd watched the fight in their hotel and afterwards made their way to the arena where they tried to get in to see me, but a burly security guard refused them access, even though they had proper passes. When an argument broke out the guard threatened to call police and have them arrested. Eventually, common sense prevailed and they were allowed in, but the incident just added insult to injury.

After everything that had happened, Linda and I and the kids all looked forward to heading off on holiday. A family fortnight in Disneyworld would help heal the wounds, physical as well as emotional.

I needed a bit of time and space to consider my boxing future.

A Sickening Night

It was time to take stock. I was just short of my 30th birthday. It had taken me an awful long time to get a crack at the world title and I worried that at my age I was running out of time for another attempt. There was no chance I would get a quick rematch for the WBC crown, thanks to those 12th round knock-downs. Had I stayed on my feet I reckon there would have been an automatic return fight, but the way things panned out Whitaker could claim he had nothing left to prove against me. I was still angry at the way the judges marked the contest. I reckoned they were so in awe of Whitaker, they gave him far too much credit for inconsequential actions, while ignoring much of my good work.

In the immediate aftermath I was psychologically down and my body was sore from all the punches I took. But now, after a family holiday in Florida, the pain and the clouds in my head were receding. I knew I was good enough to beat at least one of the other current champs and I decided to focus on the WBO's Eamonn Loughran. There was a very strong reason for choosing him. I reckoned the man from Northern Ireland would be the easiest to beat. I reckoned the European title I held was more prestigious than his world crown and most observers agreed with me.

I had previously described the WBO as a Mickey Mouse outfit but I was so desperate to be the world champion, I was prepared to eat my words for a crack at their belt. Mickey Duff, who reckoned I didn't disgrace myself in Atlantic City, was keen to set up the showdown but he knew it wouldn't happen overnight. Consequently, plans were made for an easy comeback fight for me. I was set to face Benji Marquez, a journeyman from Denver, Colorado, at the Kelvin Hall on

18th October while I waited on the outcome of negotiations with Loughran's management.

One potential fly in the ointment, however, was the appearance on the scene of Gary Murray, the Scottish welterweight who was fighting out of South Africa. By amazing coincidence, on the day I lost to Whitaker he won the vacant World Boxing Union Welterweight title. His triumph almost went un-noticed, which isn't entirely surprising since it took place in the far-from-glamorous Village Green in Durban, South Africa. And he, too, wanted to challenge Loughran. In fact, it transpired he'd been chasing a showdown with the WBO champ for some time and two proposed fights between them had fallen through. Now, as a world champion in his own right, Gary Murray believed he could not be denied any longer. But it was another Murray, James, who soon made the headlines and, tragically, for all the wrong reasons.

I first came across him in April 1994 when he was on the undercard for my victory over Allesandro Duran at the Kelvin Hall. He beat Peter Buckley, a journeyman from Birmingham, on points over six three-minute rounds. It was his eighth win in nine fights and there was no doubt he had a promising career ahead of him as a bantamweight. Incidentally, if you've ever wondered about the meaning of the term "journeyman" then a glance at Buckley's record will reveal all. He began his career in 1989 and didn't retire until 2008. During those 19 years he fought all over the UK and occasionally abroad. He must have loved it because he lost far more often than he won. By the time he hung up his gloves he'd racked up 300 pro fights, winning just 32, drawing 12 and losing 256 times. His longest losing run lasted just over three years, from July 2005 till September 2008, and consisted of 47 fights. Buckley drew his next bout then lost twice before winning and immediately quitting (on a rare high) on 31st October 2008. As I said at the start of this book, all boxers are brave and Peter "The Professor" Buckley must be one of the bravest to carry on suffering all that punishment for so long. I take my hat off to him and others like him without whom the fight game wouldn't be what it is.

James Murray was in a different league to Peter Buckley. After defeating him he kept winning and on 18th November 1994 he beat Shaun Anderson for the vacant Scottish Bantamweight title. Murray remained undefeated through three more fights and then he faced fellow Scot Drew Docherty for the British title. Docherty, from Condorrat, was the holder and a class act. In just his ninth fight he had taken the title from Joe Kelly (having already beaten Peter Buckley twice). Three more victories followed, including a third against Buckley, and Docherty was soon in the ring at the Kelvin Hall against Vincenzo Belcastro for the European title. It was 2nd February 1994, the day after I successfully defended my Euro crown against Kalankete in France. Yet, despite home advantage, Docherty failed to dethrone the Italian, who was making his third successful defence. That setback, a unanimous points decision, didn't halt Docherty's progress and just 12 months later he was considered good enough to challenge Alfred Kotey for his WBO world title.

Kotey "The Cobra", from Ghana, was making the second defence of the belt he'd won seven months earlier. The fight took place in Docherty's backyard, the Tryst Sports Centre in Cumbernauld, but the venue didn't provide any advantage because it was all over a minute into the fourth round, the champ retaining his title with a TKO. And so, after aiming for the stars perhaps too soon, Docherty's management brought their man down to earth with a British title defence against James Murray on 13th October 1995 at the Hospitality Inn, Glasgow. I was ringside with my dad. About an hour before the fight I had a few minutes with James and wished him luck. A few hours later he was dead.

Most observers reckoned Murray may have had a slight lead going into the final round of a very close encounter.

With 34 seconds left in the 12th Docherty knocked him to the canvas with a good punch. James lost consciousness and was rushed to hospital where he was pronounced dead. A post mortem revealed he'd developed a blood clot in the brain, probably around the time of the sixth round. It was a tragic night, which became a crazy night when a bunch of drunken hooligans started fighting at ringside while James lay battling for his life. The shameful scenes were captured by TV cameras and those of us watching were shocked beyond belief.

In the days leading up to James' funeral I came under immense public pressure to quit boxing. My family were all over the papers. First of all my father was interviewed and he said: "You always fear something terrible could happen and I would be happy to see Gary pack in boxing. Now the tragedy of James Murray has brought it all so much closer to home I feel very sad. The majority of boxers will tell you that they aren't going out to deliberately hurt one another but the aim is to beat your opponent and if you stop him it gets the job done quickly. If a fighter loses, his pride is hurt. But you recover from wounded pride and I am always delighted so long as Gary's physically okay after a fight. I've been telling Gary to pack it in since the Whitaker fight."

My wife, Linda, used to watch all my fights, either live or on TV. But that all changed when I got caught by Mickey Hughes in 1990. She was very upset and after that she refused to watch me at all. She would get so uptight and nervous, she couldn't even bring herself to be in the hall for my world title clash. The day after the death of James Murray I promised her I would quit if I lost my next world title fight. I knew she had wanted me to retire for some time and this was a way of finding a compromise. Linda was next to be interviewed by the press and she told a reporter: "I was half asleep when he came home (from the Murray fight) but I was aware of him standing there for some time looking at me in bed with the girls, they had wanted to sleep with me that night. He just stood there quietly then went downstairs. He loves the girls (Olivia and Jenna) dearly and I think this tragedy has hit very close to home. He thinks now about what would happen if he never saw his kids again.

"I have wanted Gary to quit for a long time because of the dangers. But I know he will not retire until at least the next world title fight. He is driven by ambition to be the best. He loves his sport and he is super fit. It is nothing to do with the money. We have a lovely five-bedroom house now. But I know I will continue to suffer, to have nightmares about the outcome of every fight. Our phone has not stopped ringing since Friday, with Gary's pals asking why he doesn't quit now. If I gave him an ultimatum he would probably quit now. But he would be completely miserable. We are in a Catch-22 situation. Although I go through hell when Gary is fighting, I'd also like to see him win a world title. But it is a two-edged sword for all of us when he steps into that ring. Will Gary be hurt, even die? Or will he be responsible for the death of another boxer? That would be like murder. I don't know how we would live with something like that for the rest of our lives."

I had been in training for my next fight against Benji Marquez and now I took a couple of days off to reflect. My father had never been happy with me as a boxer so his reaction wasn't new. This time, though, his quit plea to me was more heartfelt because he had been so close to the tragedy as it unfolded. Linda had also been hinting for a while that I should consider a different career path and she had become more vocal since Olivia and Jenna were born. I didn't blame her, she was a loving mother concerned for her family's future happiness and wellbeing.

The trouble was, I didn't know anything else. And deep down I, along with every other boxer, knew that statistically the fight game wasn't that dangerous. As I said to one reporter: "More people died on the Scottish mountains last year than in the past 50 years of professional boxing." So I told the world

I would carry on.

At this stage I was more worried about the effect of the tragedy on Drew Docherty than my own safety and as things panned out my concern was not misplaced. Drew, who was a placid type outside the ring, retired five years later. He fought just six times after the Murray fight, winning only once. I'm convinced the terrible events of that night had a major impact on his career. The incident caused boxing promoter Frank Warren to create the Murray Stone foundation to ensure all boxers were given an MRI scan to maintain their health. In addition, Britain's Board of Control published a 12-point plan to increase safety in the ring, based on a report by an independent panel of neurosurgeons. More emphasis was placed on the effects of dehydration which is believed to have played a significant role on the death of James Murray and Bradley Stone a year earlier.

Claude Abrams summed things up perfectly when he wrote in *Boxing News*: "Boxing is becoming tougher, men are getting fitter and punching harder. Under these conditions the more medical provisions, the better." Eventually the Board of Control decided that all professional fighters must pass an annual MRI brain scan.

Making the Weight

I DON'T KNOW WHAT happened to Benji Marquez, but he suddenly dropped out with two days to go and Londoner Leigh Wicks stepped in at the last minute. It didn't really make any difference to me because I was being lined up for an easy victory as part of my comeback. Leigh was another of the great journeymen in British boxing who would happily fill a gap on a promoter's bill at short notice. He was just a few months older than me yet would continue fighting right up until near his 40th birthday. To be fair, the final six years of his career weren't much to write home about — he lost 50 of his last 51 fights, including twice to one Lester Jacobs, who, as far as I know, isn't a relative. So while his career never hit the heights, Leigh, and many others like him, are an indispensable part of the game and deserve our admiration and gratitude.

Leigh wasn't a stranger to Glasgow, or me. He'd fought there in 1992 on the undercard of my British title triumph against Del Bryan, so he knew what to expect. Our fight on 18th November 1995, lasted just three of the scheduled ten rounds when he retired after damaging his left hand. I was well on top and although on paper the result was never in doubt, there were some doubts in the back of my mind beforehand. I knew if I lost to a lucky punch my career would be over. Instead, I was now brimming with confidence and demanding a showdown with Eamonn Loughran. I issued a public challenge to him but it looked as if he was avoiding me. I didn't blame him. I don't think anybody in their right minds would relish the prospect of taking on anyone who lasted the distance with Whitaker.

And for as long as I wasn't the number one challenger (I

was number five with all the boxing rankings), he could refuse to face me. If I became number one he would have to make a mandatory defence against me. Mickey alluded to that when he remarked: "Common sense says Loughran should fight Gary at the first available opportunity, but we're not going to wait forever. If Gary has to knock over a few guys to become number one challenger then so be it."

Over the next few months Loughran made all the right noises about taking me on in the Battle of Britain but nothing happened. Meanwhile I was training as if the fight was a done deal. By January I reckoned I could step into the ring against him at a month's notice. I was getting frustrated because I knew I was the better fighter and beating Loughran might help me get another crack at Whitaker. I really felt I was good enough to mix it regularly at that level and I wanted to be there. It wasn't about the money, although that would be good, it was more about the buzz. Nothing could match the high of fighting for a world title. However, there was plenty of competition and I needed to do something spectacular, like beat a champion, to get noticed.

Eventually, in what was a very uncharacteristic outburst, I accused Loughran of cowardice. I gave the *Daily Record* an interview and in it I launched a tirade against him. It was only the second major public rant of my career (the first was against George Collins) and it shows how desperate I was to get back into the big time. "I expected pen to have been put to paper for this fight long ago and I'm getting a bit fed up that nothing has been put on the table. He's running scared as far as I can see," I said, "Loughran certainly likes to talk about boxing and I've been reading everywhere about how much he wants to take me on. Well, I'll fight him anywhere anytime. Let's get it on and we'll both make lots of money. He should stop shouting his mouth off. If he thinks he's so good why doesn't he fight me? Then we'll see who's the best.

"Loughran has made five defences of his title but he's

fought nobodies. I don't know what his problem is. He seems to want to earn his money the easy way. He needs recognition and I can put him on the map. I'm already on the world stage and he wants to be there so what's the hold-up? Loughran has been a world champion for over a year but nobody knows who he is. He's still trying to make a name for himself and the best way is to take a big fight. My biggest worry now is that someone else gets there first and beats Loughran before he fights me. Loughran should realise he's got to put up or shut up soon. The TV companies don't want to know him but they want this fight because it would be meaningful for British fans. If it's credibility Loughran wants he should get in the ring with me."

There was no response from the Northern Irishman's camp. A few weeks later my mood brightened considerably when Linda gave birth to our son, Greg. Once again I was at Rutherglen Maternity to witness the great event. Our daughters, Olivia and Jenna, were now three and two years old and Greg's arrival, on 4th February 1996, completed the set as far as we were concerned.

After the celebrations it was back to the gym. Mickey Duff had decided to get me a crack at the Euro title I'd given up after three successful defences in order to prepare for the Whitaker fight. We both wanted you-know-who, who had been offered £100,000 to fight me, but there were no positive signs from his corner, so this was Plan B. The reigning European Champion was Frenchman Patrick Charpentier. I would take him on in France, a place which held no fears for me. Before that, though, I had a warm-up against tough Panamanian Edwin Murillo, the current holder of the IBF Inter-Continental Welterweight crown.

Murillo was in good form, having lost just one of his last ten fights, and he had immediately avenged that defeat soon after. So facing him was a bit of a risk, but I knew I had to take some chances to re-establish my reputation. I also knew that if I just went looking for easy victories I'd be doing the exact thing I'd attacked Loughran for doing. The good news about the Murillo fight, scheduled for Wednesday 13th March, was it would be screened live by the BBC. Not only would that add cash to the pot, it would give me the chance to show everyone just how good I still was.

Ranked at number three by the IBF, two above me, by beating Murillo I would expect to move above him in the ratings, thus opening up a crack at the world title held by the great Felix Trinidad. My only regret was that this fight would take place in London's Brent Town Hall, not Glasgow.

The BBC deal should have alerted Loughran's management to the potential interest in a clash with me. I was top of the bill against a relative unknown and it would be shown live. Imagine how much hype there would be from the TV people in a Battle of Britain? Despite that wake-up call there was no move from him.

In stark contrast to Loughran's silence, Murillo's manager had plenty to say pre-fight, "Murillo's in storming form, as he showed in getting the title back. Now we are going on to world honours at Jacobs' expense." And his 28-year-old protégé added: "The IBF rank me at number three and Jacobs is below. I should be higher but it shows I'm a better bet than Jacobs."

Twenty-four hours later they were both eating their words. Midway through the fifth, after softening him up with constant body shots, I floored the champ with a left hook to the head which sent him reeling to the canvas. As he tried desperately to regain his feet by pulling on the ropes the ref counted him out. It had been one way traffic right from the start, when I connected with a ferocious right hook to his body almost immediately after the first bell. In fact, I landed seven jabs on him without reply before his mind began to focus on the job. Throughout the next two rounds he tried to stop me from landing a punch, mainly by hanging on. But I kept pressing forward and eventually got through with a cracking left hook near the end of the third. In that round Murillo went down but the ref decided he'd slipped, which was the correct ruling. Then I trapped him on the ropes, landing at least five big punches from all angles. It should have been all over but he was saved by the bell. The pattern continued in the next two rounds until Murillo, who'd been virtually a spectator at his own destruction, could withstand no more punishment. He hadn't been stopped like that for over three years and the IBF bosses who were sitting ringside must have been impressed. I was now their Inter-Continental Welterweight Champion – the sixth title of my career and it was so easy, it felt as if I was the champ and he was the challenger. Yet Murillo was no mug. I was just far too good for him.

A young Joe Calzaghe was on the undercard that night, comfortably beating one Anthony Brooks. Just over a month later he won the British Super Middleweight title from the undefeated Mark Delaney. Joe continued winning for the next 12 years and retired unbeaten after 46 fights. During his career he held the world title for an incredible 11 years.

One of the criticisms levelled at me in the wake of the Whitaker fight was that I didn't make enough good use of my left hand. In fact against Sweet Pea I hardly raised it at all. So, during training since then I spent a great deal of time practising with the left and when I finally unleashed my new weapon against Murillo it worked a treat.

I had exactly three months to perfect my new move and get it ready for what I expected would be a tougher task against Charpentier. Taking his Euro title from him in his own backyard was the next step in my plan for world domination. I couldn't wait to get there, not least because my pals in French TV yet again came up with plenty of money to lure me over. Ever since I beat Proto, then defended my title twice over there, I had become a big draw in France. Now they were prepared to pay me £80,000 to cross the Channel. I'm not sure if it was because they liked me so much or because they were desperate to find a Frenchman who would finally beat me.

Unbeknown to me, there was one dark cloud on the horizon. The weigh-in took place 24 hours before the Murillo bout and I comfortably made the 10 stone 7lbs limit by a couple of pounds. Yet when I weighed myself just before entering the ring I was up at 11 stone 6 lbs. I don't think I had ever been so heavy before a fight. I didn't realise it at the time, but my body was beginning to change, and there was nothing I could do to prevent it from happening. It wouldn't be long before my weight began to affect my performance.

Dunkirk Spirit

ON SATURDAY 13TH APRIL 1996 I travelled to Liverpool to take in Eamonn Loughran's title defence against Mexican Jose Luiz Lopez. Fellow Scot Paul Weir was also on the bill. He was hoping to regain the WBO Light Flyweight title he'd lost five months earlier to Baby Jake Matlala and I was there to support him. It turned out to be an unlucky night for both of us. Lopez was a dangerous bet for Loughran. The man from Northern Ireland usually lined up opponents that his management believed would lead to easy victories, but this was a mandatory defence against the Number One challenger and Loughran had nowhere to hide. On paper Lopez was a bit of an unknown quantity and, therefore, could not be easily written off.

The Mexican had fought only once outside his home country in 40 previous bouts, but he'd won 36 of them, losing three and drawing one. It was a very good record, even if the vast majority of his victims were unknown. The one worrying statistic was the number of knock-outs he'd dished out – 26. That was twice as many as Loughran had managed and should have set off alarm bells within the champion's camp, but it didn't. Certainly Lopez wouldn't have been my first choice for an easy pay packet.

And so it proved. Loughran was knocked down three times within the first minute of the first round and after just 51 seconds of the fight his reign as world champion was over. My biggest fear had come to pass. Someone else had got to Loughran first and brutally exposed the frailties and limitations we all suspected he possessed before I could do it. To make matters worse, Paul Weir also lost, although that came as no great surprise considering the quality of the opposition.

The result at the Everton Park Sports Centre left me without a potentially lucrative Battle of Britain world title fight. I'm not sure it would ever have happened because the man from Ballymena clearly wasn't in my league and I think everybody knew that. Still, it was worth trying to set it up and full marks to Mickey for putting in so much effort. Loughran must have realised there was no way back after this defeat because he promptly retired at the relatively tender age of 26.

Despite that disappointment I still had my Euro title clash against Patrick Charpentier to look forward to. And it assumed even greater significance, as if it wasn't important enough, when the world rankings were published at the beginning of June 1996. The IBF listed me as the Number One challenger to Felix Trinidad. I knew if I disposed of Charpentier I would be in line for another crack at the world title. But a Dunkirk defeat would allow the Frenchman to take my place. In effect the 14th June showdown, my 50th pro contest, would be an unofficial eliminator for the world title. And it would determine whether my next appearance after Charpentier would be worth £5,000 or £300,000.

As usual, the French promoters were doing their bit to make life difficult for me. I'd been given three different dates for the fight. First it was 31st May, then 26th May and finally 14th June. Presumably they thought that might interrupt my training schedule. I've no doubt Charpentier knew the correct date all along and in my younger days this might well have rattled me — but I was 30 now and had seen worse shenanigans during my 11 years as a pro.

The only real concern I had was that the new date meant the fight would take place during the European Football Championship and that could mean my performance being overshadowed by the England v Scotland game at Wembley on the 15th June. In any event, my routine was unaffected. I'd always been a good trainer and that hadn't changed. I would be ready for Charpentier, any day of the week.

My confidence was back to its peak. I was even sharper and fitter than before the Murillo fight. I'd learned a great deal from the defeat to Whitaker and I was desperate to put my knowledge and experience to good use. I was determined not just to regain the crown I'd relinquished two years earlier to focus on the world title, but to win it back in style. My aim was to knock out the champ so my name and performance would become the topic of conversation among boxing aficionados around the world. Unfortunately, Charpentier knocked me out and I became the topic of conversation for all the wrong reasons! It was an unbelievable end to a fight which had started so well for me.

I spent the first three rounds sizing up my opponent. Looking at his record in the run-up to the bout, it was clear he hadn't faced any world class opposition. But there were danger signs. He'd won 21 fights with all but two inside the distance. So even though he'd beaten a bunch of nobodies, it was clear he packed a punch. I needed to be cautious and not give him the opening to land a killer blow.

By the fourth round I knew I could take him and I started piling on the pressure. In the fifth my pinpoint accuracy resulted in a huge cut on his left eyebrow. In the next round I kept on aiming for, and hitting, his face and torrents of blood were gushing from the wound. At that stage I was cruising to victory and few in the arena gave the champ a chance. The ref must have been weighing up the possibility of ending the contest, with so much blood pouring out of him. His corner must have told him he was so far behind on points, the only way he could win would be by knocking me out and he took the message to heart because as the bell for the seventh sounded he erupted across the ring and caught me with a right-left combination to the head which left me slightly stunned. He followed up with a flurry of big punches, forcing me to cling to the ropes. The ref gave me a mandatory eight count before allowing the fight to continue.

Charpentier, who just a short time earlier had been in a desperate position, realised it was now or never if he wanted to triumph and piled in with big shots from every direction and before I knew it I was down on the canvas. I clambered to my feet at the count of six and he was all over me again. I was trying desperately to defend myself against this ferocious onslaught and within myself I reckoned I could make it till the end of the round. The ref didn't agree and suddenly he stepped in to stop the fight. It was a disastrous end to what had begun as such a promising night. It also meant that, after years of trying, the French finally got their revenge for all the humiliation I had heaped on their champions.

Afterwards, I hinted to the press that my days as a welterweight were probably over. It was becoming increasingly difficult to make the 10st 7lbs target and the effort involved had probably contributed to my demise. Having said all that I still believe Charpentier got lucky, and I think he was aware of it, too. He carried on fighting and easily beating half-a-dozen unknowns for a couple of years before losing in three rounds to Oscar De La Hoya and promptly retiring after his one big pay-day.

As for me, I was bitterly disappointed. The chance to fight for the world title against Felix Trinidad was gone. Charpentier was now the Number One contender. But what really depressed me was the realisation that I would miss out on a rematch with Pernell Whitaker. By now I'd had a chance to analyse the raw statistics from our contest. It should have made grim reading for me as not only did he beat me, he had out-performed me in every way.

Whitaker threw a total of 667 punches to my 496 during the 12 rounds. He connected with 298 for a 45% success rate. I connected with 186, which was only 38%. He threw 254 jabs to my 179 and connected with 116 for a 46% success rate. My figures were 63 and 35%. The final set of figures concerned power punches and once again Sweet Pea was superior. He launched 413 power punches of which 182 (44%) hit their target. I, meanwhile, threw 317 and 123 (39%) were successful. So I had been outclassed in every department. A lesser mortal may have been undeterred, but not me.

A month before the ill-fated Charpentier showdown I told *Scotland on Sunday*: "I believe I am the best in the world and the only way to prove that is to beat Whitaker. I roughed him up last time and let it slip. But I'm different and he knows it. I don't take any notice of that crap about him being invincible. Everyone is invincible until I hit them on the chin.

"I'm not like Bruno against Tyson. I won't freeze on the night, because I couldn't bear the shame of letting all my friends and family down. Title chances are rare at this level so you damn well take them when they come along. I've always been that way. I've been in there with the guys who are the blue-eyed boys like Georgie Collins and I have broken them in half."

By now Linda and I and the children were living in a plush home in the upmarket Glasgow suburb of Newton Mearns, where I had spent part of my upbringing. My bank account was heavily in the black. I was driving a Porsche and had a Merc in the garage, but these material items were of little consequence to me. I dreamt of glory, as I told the paper: "I've got money coming out of my ears but I'm not satisfied because I haven't won the world title which I believe is my right and my retirement present to myself and my family. The Whitaker fight just underlined how close I am."

Sadly, those dreams were destroyed in Dunkirk.

Hanging up the Gloves

FOR THE FIRST 30 YEARS of my life things were okay; I had my ups and downs like everyone else, but I really couldn't complain. There were plenty of times when things didn't go my way, in and out of the ring, but I would always fight back and make them right. Fighting back was my destiny and by now I had grown to accept it.

As 1996 drew to a close there was not even a hint of a warning of the devastation that would shortly come to wreak havoc and destruction on me and my family. I'd just celebrated my 31st birthday and, until then, despite various setbacks, my career and life had been on an upward curve. I'd had 50 fights as a welterweight, winning all but seven. It was a good career and I reckoned it could continue to be good, even though it was time for a change of direction.

Six months earlier I had lost to Patrick Charpentier while fighting for the European Welterweight title. On the surface, succumbing to the Frenchman appeared to have dealt a fatal blow to my ambitions, but my inner desire to become world champion was as strong as ever. The Dunkirk debacle ruled out certain paths to the title but I was sure another route would come my way. I just needed to find it. So I took a few months off to think. I may have been down but I was certainly not out, although it would be nine months before I'd fight again.

Money wasn't a problem, at least not for the foreseeable future, thanks to my world title clash with Pernell Whitaker. Although at my age I was no longer a spring chicken in the fight game, thoughts of retiring hadn't even entered my head. True, my body was beginning to slow down a little, but my boxing brain was as sharp as ever. Now, early in 1997, I developed what I thought was a good plan of action. First, I decided to bow to what many saw as the inevitable and move up a weight division. It would be a lot easier to make the light-middleweight maximum of 11st than the 10st 7lbs I'd been used to throughout my career. A number of people close to me reckoned I should have done this immediately after the Whitaker defeat, but I was getting plenty of good purse offers at welterweight and it was impossible to turn them down. I did harbour hopes of returning to the welterweight division at some stage in the future but it was not a priority.

I half wondered if my weight issues had been compounded by all the chocolate I'd eaten. Most people who were close to me knew I was a chocoholic and stuffed my face with the stuff after every fight. It was my main vice – I didn't drink, gamble or smoke. But what only a few close friends knew is that I would normally cram a whole load of chocolate down my throat immediately after the weigh-in. I used to have a never-ending supply of the biggest Dairy Milk bars available just for these occasions. I thought if I could conquer my chocolate addiction it would help me lose weight.

I also started working under the influence of a new trainer. I'd first met Dean Powell in 1987 when I worked out at the famous Thomas a Beckett gym in London. He became the manager there that year at aged just 22. Now, nine years later, we hooked up again and he became my guiding light. After watching me in the gym a few times he told me there wasn't much he could teach me. He said I knew what I had to do and that he would act as an adviser and work with me to get my career back on track. Dean was my age and we got on well together. So much so, we struck up a close friendship which lasted until his tragic death in September 2013.

The comeback fight he and my manager Mickey Duff arranged for me was against Jimmy Vincent in London's Lewisham Theatre on 25th March 1997. Vincent had a reasonable record of 16 wins and eight losses and although this was my light-middleweight debut, I wasn't too concerned about taking him on. Dean was responsible for hand-picking my opponents and I trusted his judgement. And so it proved, although I got a fright early on in the first round when he stunned me with a good left hook. It wasn't enough to put me down and just before the end of the round I caught him with a peach of a right. I knew he was in trouble and moved in for the kill. I had him on the ropes and he couldn't defend himself. His knees buckled and the ref stepped in to check him out. From the restart I smashed a right cross into his face. He went down but got up only to face a new barrage of blows. I threw a couple of heavy punches without reply and the ref decided he'd seen enough. It was all over, much to Jimmy Vincent's disgust. Frankly, I don't know what he was complaining about. If the fight had gone on any longer he would have spent a fair amount of time in hospital!

It was a cool, professional performance on my part, bolstered by a full-on training routine that had Dean Powell drooling. When I went to the gym it was like going to a full-time job. I got organised and started working as quickly as possible. I didn't talk to anyone, most of the time I didn't even say hello to anyone. I just got on with it as best I could – and that meant seriously hard work. Dean used to tell the youngsters to watch me and learn. He wanted them to follow my example and become as disciplined and dedicated as I was. I was so fit and comfortable at my new weight, and the Vincent fight had taken so little out of me, it was decided to arrange my next bout as quickly as possible. It came in the shape of Viktor Fesechko from the Ukraine.

Like Jimmy Vincent, Fesechko was a bit of an unknown quantity, with most of his fights taking place in his home country, He had a positive win ratio and, therefore, had to be respected, but not feared. So, just 22 days after my last fight on 16th April 1997, I was back in action again. This time we'd moved to York Hall in London's Bethnal Green. Like the Vincent fight it was scheduled for eight rounds, but this time I was forced to go the distance. I was surprised by that because I was feeling very strong and confident. Having said that, until our bout, my opponent had never been counted out, so he was clearly a tough customer. Although I had predicted I would knock him out in four or five rounds, I had to settle for a comprehensive victory in which I didn't lose a round. My confidence, which had been shaken after losing to Charpentier, continued to improve after this result and I seriously started thinking about fighting for a world crown again. I was feeling much more comfortable at this new weight, but it still wasn't quite right. So it was decided my next fight would be at middleweight.

By now the IBF had me ranked in the top 10 of the Middleweight Division and Mickey Duff, working with promoter Frank Maloney, arranged for me to take on Russia's Yuri Epifantsev for the vacant Intercontinental title on 12th July. This belt was for boxers ranked within the top 10. Winning it could be a big step towards a world title fight. I was on the undercard for the clash between Herol 'Bomber' Graham and Chris Johnson for the vacant World Boxing Council International Super Middle Title. Bomber won comfortably with a TKO in the eighth of 12 rounds. He retained his title six months later then lost to Charles Brewer for the IBF Super-Middleweight title in March 1998. Like me he had won the British, Commonwealth and European titles while losing out for the world crown, but that is where any similarities ended. Herol retired from the ring after the Brewer fight but has continued to face major battles in his personal life. He was treated for depression and bipolar disease. This has led to him being held in a secure mental health unit on suicide watch. On one occasion he was Sectioned when he slit his wrists after drinking a bottle of brandy.

Herol's story is similar to that of many ex-fighters who were physically and mentally damaged as a consequence of the punches they took. Some ended up severely traumatised, impoverished and suffering from serious mental health issues. Others, like undefeated world champ Joe Calzaghe, have since admitted that they turned to cocaine to, in his own words, "fill in the long days since my retirement". Former world champion Ricky Hatton needed rehab for drink and depression after retiring in 2012. He revealed that at one time he didn't care if he lived or died, saying, "Depression is hard to describe unless you've been through it. You need help but you don't want to tell anyone. You're in bed crying every day. I wouldn't wish it on my worst enemy."

In the days leading up to the Epifantsev fight I was certainly feeling depressed about my own situation. There were two problems monopolising my mind. The fight was coming round too soon for my liking, less than three months after the Fesechko fight. It meant I'd have three contests in the space of four months, which, at my age, was a bit much even for a super fit training fanatic like me. In addition, I was still having issues with my weight. These thoughts were going through my head as I readied myself for my next challenge. It was hardly the ideal mental or physical preparation for such an important event. But I couldn't turn down the opportunity. It may never present itself again.

As the big night at London's Olympia approached, I knew deep inside that I wasn't at my best. I was a bit battle-fatigued and struggled slightly to make the weight, although I managed it. Despite that I was full of my usual pre-fight bravado. I certainly didn't want to give my opponent any clues about my mental and physical state so, on the eve of the showdown, I told a reporter, "I'm going to be world champion. I haven't got a negative thought in my head. I don't talk about if I win the world title, I say when I win it. Once I've beaten Epifantsev my next fight will be a world title bout and I don't care who it's against. It doesn't make a jot of difference to me whether it's for the WBA, WBC, WBO or IBF title. I want to fight the first guy who is available. And once I've won the title I'll take it from there. I might even say that's it, I've had enough. I've reached my goal. I've been about for a long time and maybe it will be the case that I can't be bothered any more. The one thing that is certain right now is that this is one of the biggest fights of my career. It's like being in the final stretch. I can't afford to slip up so close to the finishing line. I can't be beaten. But then I'm in great shape. I've never felt better, sharper or fitter. I don't expect to get it easy, but Epifantsev must realise he's going in against a guy who knows he can't lose."

It was a different story I told to Dean Powell as I stepped into the ring: "Whatever happens tonight, win or lose, this is it. This is my last fight."

In truth, I was really tired and fed up. I should have been on holiday somewhere re-charging my batteries. Instead I was facing a rugged Russian who wanted to knock my head in. Two things kept me going that night – my survival instinct and my pride. I didn't want to get hurt and I didn't want to let anyone down. I still wanted to win and I thought I would probably do so, but the old desire was missing.

The bookies, unaware of my inner turmoil, made me the red hot favourite to make it three victories in a row. So it was a big shock to everyone (except me) when I lost a unanimous points decision. Epifanstev was nothing special. Some commentators described him as a journeyman, although he was much better than that. Had I been firing on all cylinders he would have been very lucky to survive 12 rounds with me. He was comprehensively taken apart in his next two contests by two top-class fighters – Englishman Ryan Rhodes, one of my former sparring partners before he went on to greater glory, and Markus Beyer from Germany – before his career went in to serious decline. In the run-up to his retirement in 2001 he lost five of the last six fights against poor opposition. Yet I had been beaten by him. I had been slow and uninspired and, once again, troubled by my weight without really understanding why.

Afterwards my despondency was there for all to see. Under the headline "Down and Out" an interview I gave to *The Sun* perfectly summed up my mood: "I'm now thinking along the lines of chucking it. I've had a good career but there comes a stage when you wonder if you've gone to the well once too often. I struggled against a guy who is a mediocre fighter. Epifantsev certainly isn't world-class and I shouldn't be having trouble with fighters of his standard. But don't ask me why I lost. I just know that I couldn't move up a gear. I even asked myself at the end of the eighth round what I was doing in the ring."

Dean Powell had a different take on it. A few years later he told me, "Towards the end, because you had disciplined yourself for such a long time, you thought since you had moved up to light middleweight it was a licence for you to eat and drink whatever you wanted. This was your body rebelling against you because you'd starved it for so long to make the weight at welter. It happened to lots of fighters. Thomas Hearns started off at welter and ended up a cruiser where the limit's 14st 4lb.

"The timing of the weigh-in was also critical. This one was at 4pm and the fight didn't start till 8pm the next night. You had 28 hours to eat and drink without worrying about it. You didn't eat a load of junk. You thought you were doing the right thing but you weren't because you got in the ring at a weight you were not naturally comfortable with. A hungry fighter is a good fighter but you weren't hungry. When you stepped in to the ring you were well over 12 stone. I reckon you might have been as high as 12st 6lb. You were as fat as anything. I heard one guy in the crowd say, 'he's got bigger tits than my wife'. You were just too heavy to fight and you just couldn't do it. He didn't beat you. You lost because you ate your way out of the title."

As usual, Dean spoke a lot of sense. But by then it didn't matter. My boxing career had come to an ignominious end that night in London and once again it was time for a change of direction. It wouldn't be long before I'd discover that the toughest battles I'd faced in the ring were a walk in the park compared to the horrific nightmares I was about to endure.

The Fightback

AFTER THE TRIALS and tribulations of my business failure and Linda's breast cancer scare, I started thinking about getting back into boxing. The idea came to me after meeting a young Glasgow fight promoter called Sam Kynoch. I first met him at one of his boxing promotions in 2012. I had been along at the event in Scotstoun Leisure Centre as a guest. Afterwards I tried to speak to Sam, but it wasn't the right time for him that night. We met for a coffee a few days later and I told him I was interested in getting back into boxing. I thought I might do a charity exhibition bout in aid of the Beatson West of Scotland Cancer Centre, as a thank you for the great treatment my wife received there. Sam and I hit it off right from the first moment and we decided there and then we would organise an event at the Crown Plaza. Sam arranged everything. He even found me an opponent I could beat, which was no easy task considering how unfit I was, and we raised a substantial sum, in the region of £6,000, for the cancer unit. I got a massive reception from the crowd when I entered the ring. It wasn't quite like old times but it was amazing and gratifying nonetheless. I must admit, I had a sneaking fancy to try a proper fight against another ex pro if one could be found.

So many top fighters had turned their back on retirement in recent years it looked like boxing had developed a veterans circuit, much like golf's Seniors Tour. Herol Graham took four years off before making a comeback at the age of 37. During the next 12 months he won four times, picking up and defending the WBC International Super Middleweight title. He finally retired for good after losing out on another world title bid. In March 1998, at the age of 38, he was beaten by

Charles Brewer, the reigning IBF World Super Middleweight champion, the fight taking place in the same Atlantic City venue where I had lost to Whitaker.

Sugar Ray Leonard retired in 1991 and six years later, just a couple of months before his 41st birthday, he took on and lost to Hector Camacho, bringing his comeback hopes to a shuddering end. Roberto Duran, who made his pro debut in 1968, was still fighting 33 years later in 2001. By then he was 50 years old! He too lost his final fling against Camacho, who by comparison was a mere youngster at just 39. George Foreman, who was born in January 1949, initially retired in 1977 after losing to Jimmy Young, who was far from a world title contender. He became an ordained minister and launched the George Foreman Grill. George earned far more from the grill than he ever made in the fight game. Nobody knows for sure how much it was, but it is generally assumed to be around $200 million. At one stage he was reportedly being paid $8 million a month!

Despite those fabulous paydays the lure of the ring was too strong and he made his comeback nearly 10 years after he quit. Although he was now 38 years old, George turned back the clock with ease as the fights came at him thick and fast. In 1987 he won five in a row. The following year he won nine in a row. In 1989 he won another five without loss. In 1990 he took on another five opponents, none of whom lasted more than four rounds with him. His first loss on his comeback trail was in 1991 to the fists of the great Evander Holyfield who, at just 29, was 13 years his junior. At stake were the WBC, WBA and IBF World Heavyweight titles. Despite that serious age gap Foreman went the distance. Undeterred by that defeat Big George kept going. Three more victories followed before he lost to Tommy Morrison for the vacant WBO World Heavyweight title, but he bounced back by winning the WBA and IBF World Heavyweight titles against Michael Moorer in November 1994, just a couple of months short of his 46th birthday. At that point there was no stopping Big George. In 1995 he defended his IBF title and collected the vacant WBU Heavyweight belt by defeating Axel Schultz. The following year he successfully defended both against Crawford Grimsley. In 1997 he held on to his WBU title against Lou Savarese before finally calling it a day later that year after losing to Shannon Briggs. By then he was nearly 49 years old. Tommy Morrison, meanwhile, called it a day in 1996 but returned for two more fights in 2007.

Larry Holmes and Mike Weaver were another couple of ex-champs who couldn't stay away from the ring despite their advancing years. On 17th November 2000, exactly two weeks after Holmes celebrated his 51st birthday, the pair clashed in Biloxi, Mississippi. Weaver was no spring chicken at just two-and-a-half years younger than Holmes. The older man prevailed with a TKO in round six of the scheduled 10. While Weaver decided enough was enough, that triumph encouraged The Easton Assassin to make one more effort. In July 2002, and despite being nearly 53 years old, he comfortably won a unanimous decision against Eric 'Butterbean' Esch, who was almost 20 years his junior. After that the great man called it quits.

Another of the all-time greats who just couldn't hang up his gloves and quietly fade away was Carlos Palomino who, like Holmes and Foreman, was born in 1949. He made a comeback after being retired for an incredible 18 years! Palomino hit the big time at London's Wembley Arena in 1976. The tough Mexican took the WBC world Welterweight title from champion John H Stracey after knocking the Englishman to the canvas for counts of eight twice in the 12th round. Six months later, in January 1977, he defended his title in a bout which made boxing history. His opponent was fellow countryman Armando Muñíz. This clash was unique because two college graduates were facing each other for a world title for the first time. Palomino had a degree in Recreation

Administration from Long Beach State, while Muniz had graduated from California State Los Angeles, with a joint degree in Spanish and Maths. At that point he was working towards another degree in Administration. Palomino retained his title with a final round KO and went on to make six successful defences, including a re-match with Muniz, before losing to Wilfredo Benitez in January 1979. Five months later, in June 1979, Palomino lost his next fight to Roberto Durán at Madison Square Gardens, on the undercard of the Larry Holmes – Mike Weaver world Heavyweight title clash. Immediately afterwards he announced his retirement. Yet, on 10th January 1997, at the age of 48, he resumed his career by beating Ismaél Díaz by a knockout in round nine. He won four fights that year, but when he lost to Wilfredo Rivera in May 1998 he decided to retire for good.

So yes, at the age of 47 I briefly flirted with the idea of making a comeback. However, the thought of going back to a highly disciplined way of life was enough to put me off. The exhibition bout, though, was very successful so Sam and I did another one and after that I started going to Sam's gym, initially just to work out. It was nice being back in that kind of environment, among other boxers who took their sport seriously. Before long I started training more vigorously and helping out with the other boxers who worked out there under Sam's direction and by 2014 I was hooked. I became more and more involved with the training of up-and-coming boxers at the gym. Then, in 2015, I formally signed up to become a fully-fledged licenced professional trainer and became the gym's head coach.

Until that point Sam had been both managing and training the boxers who had begun to flock to his gym, but the job eventually became just too big for one man. He wanted to focus on managing and promoting so my arrival on the scene suited us both perfectly. We have a good stable, many of whom started their career with Sam. We started working together with them. I did my best to pass on all I've learned, inside and outside of the ring, to them. It would be great if, thanks to me, they avoid some of the pitfalls I fell into. And as you know there have been plenty.

Still Fighting

IN RECENT YEARS I sometimes felt that when one door was closed on me, another slammed in my face! And I couldn't help wondering if that would happen again when Sam Kynoch and I decided to go our separate ways. The split happened not long after I had helped train one of the fighters in his stable to a world title. Hannah Rankin was an excellent pupil and I was proud to be in her corner when she defeated Maria Lindbergh for the vacant WBA and IBO super welterweight titles. The fight, at the Tottenham Hotspur Stadium, took place on Guy Fawkes night 2021. The officials awarded her a unanimous points decision. Hannah is a superb athlete and also a talented musician, having become an accomplished bassoonist after studying at the Royal Conservatoire of Scotland and the Royal Academy of Music in London. We enjoyed a great relationship and after defending her titles in May 2022 I was saddened to learn she lost them a few months later.

For a short while I was at a loose end again, as far as boxing was concerned, but then a quirk of fate changed things around for me. I'd donated a prize of a personal training session with me to a charity dinner at Celtic Park and it was bought by businessman Richard Shields. I did a session with him and he introduced me to his brother Mark and before long I was training the pair regularly and we became good friends. The brothers are big fight fans and were long-term supporters of the St Andrews Sporting Club in Glasgow, which celebrated its 50th anniversary in 2023 as Scotland's premier boxing venue. They were also, crucially for me, sponsors of Martin Harkin, a tough welterweight from Dumbarton.

Martin is managed by Ian Wilson, owner of the St Andrews

Sporting Club, who I have known for many years. He took over the club from Tommy Gilmour Junior in 2014 and during that time I was a regular at the shows, often presenting the prize for Boxer of the Month. Many of the youngsters who met me on those occasions knew little about me at the time, but they soon learned when they Googled my name. On one occasion I was the guest of honour and at the 50th celebrations I was also one of the guests, alongside Jim Watt.

So, at the tail end of 2021 when it was suggested that I start training Martin, there was unanimous agreement. His first fight under my training regime was on Thursday 10th February, 2022 at Glasgow's Radisson Blu Hotel, when he took the ring with me in his corner against Ukrainian Vitalii Maksymiv. Martin was well on top and the ref stopped the fight in the third round to spare the Ukrainian further damage after he was sent to the canvas by a ferocious right hander. Martin and I kept working hard and the effort paid off in his next fight. This time Martin topped the bill at the Normandy Hotel, Renfrew. Facing him was Edvinas Puplauskas from Lithuania. Martin had his opponent down in the second round and again in the fifth before running out a comfortable points winner. His displays had obviously caught the attention of all the right people, because his next fight would be for the WBO European Welterweight Title. The 10-rounder was scheduled for the 8th October, 2022 at a packed Bolton Whites Hotel, which forms part of the Bolton Wanderers FC stadium complex. Martin was taking on the more experienced local boy Liam Taylor and unfortunately things did not go to plan and Martin was stopped in the fourth round after being knocked down three times. Despite that there wasn't a mark on him at the end and he was none the worse for wear. He was a bit disconsolate, however, but that is not surprising under the circumstances.

It wasn't long before Ian Wilson offered me the chance to train another exciting prospect from his stable. Jack Owens is unique among fighters because he was the world junior and senior kickboxing champion before he decided to step inside a boxing ring. The 24-year-old from Johnstone started fighting at the age of nine and by 15 was European Champion. A year later he had his first world title. By the end of 2016 he had won world titles at two different weights. But he always knew he wanted to move on to boxing. He had 11 fights as an amateur, losing around half of them, before turning pro.

When we first met he asked me if I would help him to make a name in the professional ranks and I was delighted to accept. His debut took place on Friday, 29th September 2023 at the Normandy Hotel, Renfrew. His opponent, Estonian Dmitri Protkunas, was no pushover. His fight against Jack was the 12th of his career and he was most certainly not there as cannon fodder! After four tough rounds Jack was the winner on points.

I was in his corner that night and was very impressed by how well he handled the pressure. His career is up and running and I reckon he could go far. I'll certainly be giving him every piece of help and advice I can and hopefully he can learn from some of my mistakes! And if he falls by the wayside, I'll be there to pick him up and dust him down.

Today, as I grow gracefully into middle age, I can look back on my life so far with a great deal of satisfaction and even pride at some of my achievements, and although much of it happened purely by accident, there is one recurring theme.

Whenever fate was unkind to me, I always fought back!

GARY JACOBS PROFESSIONAL RECORD
53 FIGHTS 45 WINS (26 KOs) 8 LOSSES (2 KOs)

www.boxrec.com

DATE	OPPONENT	VENUE	RESULT	ROUND
1997-07-12	Yuri Epifantsev	Olympia, Kensington	L-UD	12/12
		IBF Inter-Continental Middle (vacant)		
1997-04-16	Viktor Fesechko	York Hall, Bethnal Green	W-PTS	8/8
1997-03-25	Jimmy Vincent	Lewisham Theatre, Lewisham	W-TKO (1/8)	1/8
1996-06-14	Patrick Charpentier	Sportica Arena, Gravelines	L-TKO	7/12
		EBU European Welter		
1996-03-13	Edwin Murillo	Brent Town Hall, Brent	W-KO	5/12
		IBF Inter-Continental Welter		
1995-11-18	Leigh Wicks	Kelvin Hall, Glasgow	W-RTD	3/10
		Wicks retired with damaged hand		
1995-08-26	Pernell Whitaker	Convention Hall, Atlantic City	L-UD	12/12
		WBC World Welter		
1995-03-04	Jose Miguel Fernandez	Convention Center, Atlantic City	W-UD	10/10
1994-11-09	Marcelo Domingo Di Croce	London Arena, Millwall	W-PTS	10/10
1994-10-05	Rusty Derouen	Civic Hall, Wolverhampton	W-TKO	
1994-04-13	Alessandro Duran	Kelvin Hall, Glasgow	W-KO	8/12
		EBU European Welter		
1994-02-01	Tusikoleta Nkalankete	Palais des Sport Marcel Cerdan, Levallois-Perret	W-UD	12/12
		EBU European Welter		
1993-09-22	Daniel Bicchieray	Grand Hall, Wembley	W-TKO	5/12
		EBU European Welter		
		Bicchieray stopped with cut left eyebrow		
1993-05-19	Horace Fleary	Crowtree Leisure Centre, Sunderland	W-RTD	4/8
1993-02-06	Ludovic Proto	Cirque d'Hiver, Paris	W-TKO	9/12
		EBU European Welter		
1992-10-16	Ludovic Proto	Salle Pierre de Coubertin, Paris	L-SD	12/12
		EBU European Welter (vacant)		
		Jacobs docked a point in the final round.		
1992-07-09	Robert Wright	Scottish Exhibition Centre, Glasgow	W-TKO	6/12
		BBBofC British Welter		
1992-04-22	Nino Cirilo	Wembley Arena, Wembley	W-PTS	10/10
1992-03-25	Tommy Small	Royal Albert Hall, Kensington	W-TKO	2/10
1992-02-20	Del Bryan	Scottish Exhibition Centre, Glasgow	W-PTS	12/12
		BBBofC British Welter		
1991-11-20	Peter Eubanks	Royal Albert Hall, Kensington	W-PTS	8/8
1991-03-05	Kenny Louis	Hospitality Inn, Glasgow	W-KO	2/8

1990-10-17	Mickey Hughes	York Hall, Bethnal Green	L-KO	8/10
		Hughes was behind on points		
1990-05-09	Mike Durvan	Royal Albert Hall, Kensington	W-KO	1/8
1990-04-26	Pascal Lorcy	Latchmere Leisure Centre, Wandsworth	W-TKO	2/10
		Lorcy stopped with gashed upper lip		
1989-11-23	Donovan Boucher	Civic Centre, Motherwell	L-PTS	12/12
		Commonwealth Boxing Council Welter		
1989-00-27	Duddy McGirt	Felt Forum, New York	L-UD	10/10
1989-06-27	Rollin Williams	Royal Albert Hall, Kensington	W-TKO	1/10
1989-04-05	George Collins	Royal Albert Hall, Kensington	W-PTS	12/12
		Commonwealth Boxing Council Welter		
		WBC International Welter		
1989-02-14	Rocky Kelly	Latchmere Leisure Centre, Wandsworth	W-TKO	7/12
		Commonwealth Boxing Council Welter		
1988-11-29	Richard Rova	Royal Albert Hall, Kensington	W-KO	4/12
		Commonwealth Boxing Council Welter		
1988-09-16	Javier Suazo	Caesars Palace, Las Vegas	W-KO	10/12
		WBC International Welter (vacant)		
1988-06-06	Juan Alonso Villa	Hilton Hotel, Mayfair	W-TKO	5/8
1988-04-19	Wilf Gentzen	Kelvin Hall, Glasgow	W-PTS	12/12
		Commonwealth Boxing Council Welter		
1988-02-24	Del Bryan	Exhibition Centre, Glasgow	W-PTS	10/10
1987-11-26	Jeff Connors	Ramada Inn, Fulham	W-PTS	8/8
1987-06-08	Tommy McCallum	Albany Hotel, Glasgow	W-TKO	5/10
		BBBofC Scottish Area Welter		
1987-05-19	Gary Williams	Tryst Sports Centre, Cumbernauld	W-TKO	3/8
1987-04-06	Robert Armstrong	Plaza Ballroom, Glasgow	W-RTD	5/8
		Armstrong down four times and halted with left eye completely closed		
1987-02-24	Gary Williams	Plaza Ballroom, Glasgow	W-KO	7/8
		Williams down three times		
1987-01-27	Dave Douglas	Plaza Ballroom, Glasgow	W-PTS	10/10
		BBBofC Scottish Area Welter		
1986-10-20	Kelvin Mortimer	Albany Hotel, Glasgow	W-TKO	5/6
1986-09-15	Jeff Connors	Albany Hotel, Glasgow	W-TKO	3/8
1986-06-24	Dave Douglas	Plaza Ballroom, Glasgow	L-PTS	10/10
		BBBofC Scottish Area Welter (vacant)		
1986-04-14	Billy Cairns	Plaza Ballroom, Glasgow	W-PTS	8/8
1986-03-10	Alistair Laurie	Plaza Ballroom, Glasgow	W-PTS	8/8
1986-02-10	Courtney Phillips	Plaza Ballroom, Glasgow	W-TKO	5/8 x 2
		Phillips down in 5th		
1985-12-02	Dave Heaver	Plaza Ballroom, Glasgow	W-PTS	6/6
1985-11-11	Tyrell Wilson	Albany Hotel, Glasgow	W-KO	5/6
1985-10-07	Albert Buchanan	County Inn, Cambuslang	W-PTS	6/6
		Buchanan down in the 1st and 5th rounds		
1985-08-12	Mike McKenzie	Plaza Ballroom, Glasgow	W-PTS	6/6
1985-06-03	Nigel Burke	St.Andrew's Sporting Club, Glasgow	W-PTS	
1985-05-20	John Conlan	Hospitality Inn, Glasgow	W-PTS	6/6 x 2